The Parasitic Role of Elites

Why Governments, Like Soccer Matches, Need Honest Referees

With a Foreword by Jim Rumford

Award winning author of Tobacco, Trusts, And Trump:

How America's Forgotten War Created Big Government)

Lost Nation Books

Lancaster New Hampshire

A NOTE TO READERS:

This book concerns the Rise and Fall of Nations. Its conclusions are controversial. Some readers may object that there is little "theory" for we have simply compared those forms of government that worked well to those which did not. By examining the results of past experience, the reader will discover the major lessons that lie buried within this extraordinary record of human history.

Some readers may find an added degree of confidence in the findings put forth here from the fact that they have been suppressed for so long by so many: Obviously, the Truth, once exposed, will limit the power, and shred the vanity, of those who seek to rule over us.

Other readers may still, at the end, remain unconvinced about the hypotheses presented, but at least they may comprehend the inherent weaknesses of most currently popular explanations. As a minimum, it is my fervent hope that the journey will open their eyes and give them food for thought, a worthy objective for any author.

Bill Greene - (June 30, 2021)

Print ISBN: 978-1-66781-276-2
eBook ISBN: 978-1-66781-277-9

To Cathy Beautiful

OTHER BOOKS BY BILL GREENE

Wasted Genius: *How IQ & SAT Tests are Hurting Our Kids and Crippling America*, 2011

Common Genius: *Guts, Grit & Common Sense*, 2007

"Simply superb. It was hard for me to believe that there could be a totally new theory of history...But Mr. Greene ties a myriad of sources together and draws the only possible (and startlingly simple) conclusions. Kudos. Don't miss this."
Amazon Book Reviewer

"A grand revision of traditional histories that abound on the market"
Richard J. Ward, retired chairman, Economics Dept., Univ. Of Mass.

"A fascinating and clearly written book that challenges the conventional wisdom of our society's cult of expertise. It is likely to be controversial among our cultural elites."
Joseph F. Johnston, Jr., author of The Limits of Government

"Stimulating and provocative."
Brice M. Clagett, Lawyer

"Bill Greene has written a provocative book that celebrates the common sense of the people who built the West and disparages the dangerous and faulty theories of the academics who want to tear down this civilization."
Ricardo Duchesne, professor, University of New Brunswick

"The genius of this book is that it provides a compelling framework for the interpretation of history. Economic Freedom allows the Common Genius of millions of men and women to spark the human progress we all desire."
Amazon Book Reviewer

Saving Democracy! *How Good Management Could Trump Ideological Bickering*, 2016

Stories for Kids, *Outdoor Stories for Children*, 2001
(www.billgreenebooks.com)

FOREWORD

T HIS FAST PACED "STORY" BEGINS by taking readers on a whirlwind journey (beginning 5000 years ago) that examines the perpetual war between the leaders of every nation and their people. Then, using the case method, the author examines the first pioneers of democracy and why they settled in isolated and unfavorable areas, even swamps and deserts: Because that was the only way to escape oppressive elites.

This book should grab most readers' attention as they discover how those free "start-up" societies prospered for hundreds of years before an elite class gained control and imposed crippling bureaucracies and regulations. That historical record, the author explains, tells us why The Industrial Revolution occurred in Europe: Other people, all around the world, were held in oppressive autocracies with little opportunity to express their genius. The Europeans won by default!

The good news is that today, as proof of the equality of all people, we can see the spread of prosperity, liberty, and respect for human rights being enjoyed in such varied places as Singapore, Chile, Taiwan, Ghana, the Arab Emirates, and South Korea. Any people can do it—they just need the freedom to participate in their nation's affairs. The bad news is that as we look at America today, and the plight of many less developed nations, we can see a growing level of oppression and taxation that is limiting the well-being of the common people.

Readers will discover in these pages how the West got its head start and why everyone else is now catching up. It provides a remarkable wake-up call for all oppressed people to control their elite, take back their country, and gain the liberty and dignity that all people deserve.

Jim Rumford--Award winning author of *Tobacco, Trusts, And Trump; How America's Forgotten War Created Big Government*

TABLE OF CONTENTS

LIST OF ILLUSTRATIONS

PREFACE

– A Brief History of Elites & Their People

 *"The search for beginnings, no matter how far pressed, usually serves only to open more distant vistas of earlier developments."*
~~Alpheus Thomas Mason & Gordon F. Baker
Free Governments in the Making

THERE HAVE BEEN HUNDREDS OF books written by distinguished historians and economists who have attempted to explain the Rise and Fall of nations. Virtually all those books suggest that there is a cyclical pattern, beginning with an upward Rise, then a mature stage, followed by a Decline. However, none of those books have explained what causes the Rise, why they Fail, nor why some nations have fared better than others. The cause for such widely different outcomes seems to remain a mystery, but the bigger mystery is why haven't the experts come up with an explanation for what makes a nation Rise or what causes them to Decline?

Many writers have attributed a country's success to its geography, citing the importance of such features as climate, arable soil, navigable rivers, and natural resources. More recent explanations have attributed success to the social and political "conditions" of the time, or even to guns and germs, or to an "environment" that happened to be conducive to success. However, those factors are all inanimate and incapable of action. Only people can build shelters, boats, skyscrapers, and spaceships. Only people can establish a civil environment with laws, institutions, and rules that help them enjoy beneficial communities. Knowing all that, perhaps we should credit *people* for our historic innovations. Certainly, guns, environments, and arable soil can't do anything.

Searching for a correct and comprehensive answer will take us back more than 5000 years, to the time when our ancestors first settled into large communities. Prior to that time, humans lived as hunter-gatherers, living freely in small groups, with no reason to organize beyond kinship settlements. However, the Agricultural Revolution changed everything. New farm-based communities required administrators to record and manage the storage and distribution of all the expanded production.

The beginnings of the Agricultural Revolution occurred during or right after the Gobekeli Tepi (AKA Gobelki) civilization which has been recently located and unearthed in South-eastern Turkey. That civilization was populated by hunter-gatherers about 12,000 years ago and featured some of the earliest stone temples. Its megalithic rock structures were built several millennia before the 4,500-year-old pyramids in Egypt, the 5,000-year-old Stonehenge formations in England, and the 7,000-year-old Nabta Playa society. The people of Nabta Playa, located in Africa, about 700 miles south of the great Egyptian pyramids, are thought to have built the Earth's oldest astronomical observatory. It was in these earliest settled communities where people initiated the domestication of animals and the large-scale farming that fed a rapidly expanding human population.

Ever since that time, a working class of people have toiled under the supervision of their leaders, with widely varying results. Simon Sinek, an expert on leadership and corporate management, writes, "The best organizations foster trust and cooperation because their leaders build what Sinek calls a Circle of Safety (which) leads to stable, adaptive, confident teams, where everyone feels they belong, and all energies are devoted to …advance their leader's vision and their organization's interests. It's amazing how well it works… Other teams, no matter what incentives were offered, were doomed to infighting, fragmentation, and failure."[1]

The key point is that we have needed elites but should only tolerate them if they help provide us with a safe and empowering community. It is simply a bargain: tit for tat! As Sinek puts it, "There is an anthropological obligation of an alpha to protect the tribe, and in return people repaid that protection with an intense loyalty… to this day we are perfectly comfortable with the alphas…getting certain advantages. (However) the advantages of leadership do not come free… We wouldn't give them all those perks for nothing. That wouldn't be fair."[2]

Unfortunately, human nature being what it is, most leaders forget their obligations and become tyrants. The problem with such leaders was illustrated long ago by Aesop, a slave living in Greece about 2600 years ago. Among the hundreds of morality tales attributed to him was the fable entitled "Lion and Wild Ass, Partners in the Hunt."

Aesop's tale tells how a lion goes hunting with a few other animals. They all work together and are rewarded with a delicious dinner. But when they go to share the feast, the lion stops them and roars that he wants most of the spoils, and worse, he makes clear that his "partners" must wait until he has eaten his fill. The other animals, fearing the lion's wrath, meekly accept the few scraps that the lion leaves them.

That fable eventually gave birth to the expression, "the lion's share," and may have inspired the Roman lawyer, C. Cassius Longinus, around 30AD, who coined the phrase: "societas leonina" when referring to a situation where the entire profits went to some people to the exclusion of the rest.[3]

Like all fables, this one serves as a warning to us all. And its ancient origin tells us that nothing changes with human behavior and that greedy elites have plagued all the people on earth since time began! They always want to eat first and get more!

The problem with lions, and our elites, is that they are not team players. They do not want to compete on a level playing field against their fellow men and women. They get to believe that they are above the common people, that they possess special qualities that should give them a superior status. The danger they present to the common people is that they forget the bargain made. Instead, their assumed superiority justifies in their minds the right to flout the rules, to lie and cheat, to do anything, to maintain their "rightful" place on top—just like the lion, and that definitely leaves little for everyone else!

In most nations today, the elites remain focused on enriching themselves by dividing their subjects into antagonistic groupings. Instead of maintaining a "Circle of Safety," where the population is cooperative and unified, the elites do the opposite: By 1) Dividing their people, and stirring resentments, 2) creating crises as diversions, and 3) using our schools to shape the minds of our children, the elites can maintain and strengthen their position at the top. The elites don't even participate in the hunt anymore; they send the peons out to produce the bounty and just wait for them to turn most of it over to them! And they are winning: In most countries today, the people have been indoctrinated in the schools, divided into groups, fighting each other, and/or diverted by crises such as the overly hyped climate crisis, mask mandates for all, the Wuhan virus, and racism: Recently even highways have been attacked as racist!. Those diversions are designed to keep the voters from working together to fight the elites.

The only significant disagreement between the many oppressed groups is how to make the country serve all the people. Imagine what those groups could do if united and in agreement over the path forward. In this book's final chapters, the possibility of uniting all those abused members is outlined. The reality is that they are all being denied a fair share of their nation's bounty.

In brief, oppression by an elite has always been a problem for all the people in all the countries on earth. Something has to be done because too many people have been excluded, taxed, silenced, and regulated. It is the author's hope that these lessons from history's past struggles can guide all people on this abundant globe today because nothing has changed—it is simply a continuing war between elites and their people. And we need a clear and simple path forward.

This book is divided into four sections each containing four chapters:

Part I - A brief historical look at how we got here, how the elites have always ruled, usually for the worse, and how the people of a few "start-up" nations managed to build successful democracies without them. The fourth chapter reveals why the academics have failed to explain the Rise and Fall of Nations. (3000 BC to 1000 AD)

Part II – Explains the accelerating advance in technology that created modern industrial states, why they developed in only a few places, and how oppressive elites prevented freedom and progress throughout most of the world. (1000 AD to 1750 AD)

Part III – Here we examine how elites have made the simple mechanics of government and the economics of the marketplace into complicated theoretical questions: To justify their role at the top they have hidden the truth that ordinary people, relying on their innate skills and common sense, have been the builders of great nations. Chapter 9 details how our children are being "trained" and "conditioned" to defer to experts and obey authority figures. (1750 AD to 2020 AD)

Part IV – This part looks to the future, the dangerous growth of "globalist" elites, what to do about the United Nations, how to gain control over our domestic affairs, curtail foreign meddling, and unite all oppressed citizens. There is much to be done if we want our governments to work for ALL the people. Voting for leaders who will happily distribute crumbs to their supporters is not a real solution. The closing pages outline possible alternatives if we fail to take our countries back! (2020 to 2050)

THE PARASITIC ROLE OF ELITES

PART I

Why Elites Hate Governments for the People

(2000BC-1000AD)

CHAPTER 1-

The Rise and Fall of Nations— A Mystery Solved!

 *"The ultimate tragedy is not the oppression and cruelty of the bad people but the silence over that by the good people."*
Martin Luther King, Jr.

THE GARDEN OF EDEN, WHICH offered everything peaceful and bountiful for human existence, must have been a rather uneventful place before people arrived. Then, Adam and Eve, or whoever were the earliest Homo sapiens, made their appearance. Suddenly things began to pop! They built shelters, ate the low-hanging fruit, and had children, good ones and bad ones, and that's how it all began.

Prior to those first modern humans, the world's rich and arable soil, its navigable rivers, the pleasant climate, the healthy forests, and the water teeming with fish, had all lain fallow with nothing happening. If a tree fell, the silence was unbroken, for there was no one present to hear it crashing to the ground.

Archaic humans, such as Neanderthals and Homo Erectus, had lived all over the world in such surroundings for two million years "with no more impact on their environment than gorillas, fire-flies or jellyfish."[4] But then we arrived, modern men and women and everything changed. Our ancestors formed communities, built boats, traveled the world, devised machinery, split the atom, and now we are traveling in space. All in the last 10,000 years. The archaic humans had lived here a hundred times as long and done little to nothing! And all the favorable climate and geography that the Neanderthals lived in didn't accomplish anything either.

We were blessed with large and complex brains that allowed both reasoning and abstract thinking buttressed by a power for speech to communicate the resulting thoughts. The earth had never seen such competent beings before that time—new advanced beings that had the ability to totally transform their environment and reshape it into a comfortable, safe, and abundant world for their families to live in. And we did just that!

It should be self-evident that people, modern human beings just like us, built the modern world. Certainly, rivers didn't do it, nor the arable soil. The cause of all progress had to be 100 percent human action. What else could have caused the trees to be cut down, converted to lumber, and assembled into shelters and boats?

Thus, by the simple process of elimination we can solve the mystery of what determined the Rise of successful nations. There is nothing else on earth other than people that could have done it!

The more interesting mystery is why has there been so much variation around the world in the progress achieved? There are still people living in Stone Age cultures, with little or no understanding of reading and writing, arithmetic, or chemistry. And at least a billion people live in the direst poverty with little access to transportation, schooling, or modern medicine. How can that be and why haven't the experts properly explained why so many have been left so far behind?

We know from the recent and sudden success of nations all over the globe that all people have comparable abilities and potential. Colin Renfrew has confirmed that the varied histories of the world's people "cannot be explained by any inherent or emerging genetic changes…. Modern molecular genetics suggests that, apart from the normal distribution range present in all populations, in matters such as IQ, all humans are equal."[5]

As further proof, it is clear that the people of such different locales as Singapore, Japan, the Arab Emirates, Ghana, Hong Kong, Taiwan, and Chile, have all been equally adept at pursuing both the technology and the economic systems that were pioneered by Europeans. So why haven't the experts explained what held some nations back and why some others advanced so far?

Incredibly, expert historians and economists haven't even agreed that it was people that created the progress that most of us currently enjoy! In spite of their extraordinary schooling, superior academic performance, layers of advanced degrees, and years of study, they are still debating whether the development and progress of modern communities was caused by navigable rivers, or possibly guns and germs, or even by such inanimate things as forests and mineral deposits. What is wrong with them? Common sense should make it clear to everyone that rivers and mineral deposits can't do anything.

THE ORIGINS: THE HUMAN DIASPORA

In order to make sense of where we currently find ourselves and our nation, it may help to understand how we got here. History is a great teacher because just about everything that's ever happened in the social sciences has been recorded and examined since the first large communities appeared 5,000 years ago. All those communities were populated by people just like us. The best way to learn from that history is to simply study those past times and learn from all those past generations. They all had the same needs and wants as us and faced the same kinds of problems that we do.

The historical record tells us about many revolutionary leaders who have justifiably taken up arms against dictatorial elites. But sadly, the record shows that those new leaders have too often merely imposed a new oppressive regime. Both Russia and China have seen authoritarian communist leaders take control of their government during the last 100-years but retain the horrors of a totalitarian government just as evil as the one they replaced. The masses of people may hate kings and aristocracies, but they have learned also to hate misguided dictates from self-appointed saviors.

"Communism is not love. Communism is a hammer which we use to crush the enemy."

MAO ZEDONG

In this book we will search for a solution to this problem by determining what factors help shape a successful community. We have no more to do than examine the past records. Proof of what works and what fails is baked in the pudding of prior human experience. We must simply synthesize the major lessons that lie buried within the many facts of recorded human history.

Of necessity, this will be a whirlwind tour of mankind's past, but brevity is actually the best way to get the big picture without getting lost in the details. There is much wisdom to be gleaned from the past actions of individuals, the success or failure of their governments, and the successes and pitfalls they encountered. That "case method" approach will tell us what worked and what failed.

First, on the big question—Where did modern humans come from? It does not really matter for the goal of this book, so we will clip that short: Nothing provokes greater passion and anger than arguments about the origin of mankind. But no matter! It is one of those things that remains a mystery. As a good friend's priest told him, "Life is not a puzzle to be solved, but a magnificent mystery to be savored!" Nevertheless, there are at least three possible explanations for those who want to speculate on the subject:

> One, some form of aliens came to earth way back somewhere in time and messed with the genetics of the most advanced species they found and created modern man, Homo sapiens.

> Two, a Divine power, a supreme being, created life, either in the form of modern humans or as primitive cellular forms that evolved into modern men and women.

> Three, some unknown force fused the right mix of basic chemical elements in a primeval sloth until some spark ignited the broth-like recipe into a living form, a primitive amoeba, which evolved over billions of years into modern humans.

Take your pick; all three explanations seem equally implausible, and there might be a fourth. But the truth is that it does not matter for our purposes. We only want to know: How did those modern humans advance so far? At the beginning, we do know that we were living a very primitive Stone Age lifestyle.

Our direct ancestors appeared in southern Africa approximately 100,000 to 200,000 years ago. They were a new and unique form of life, possessing much greater mental and physical ability than any predecessor forms on earth. The dating estimate could be slightly different, but that isn't of critical importance either—it was very recent in geologic time.

There had already been many "archaic humans," and like most other mammals, "they loved, played, formed close friendships, and competed for status and power—but so did chimpanzees, baboons, and elephants."[6] Those archaic humans had also migrated out of Africa, dispersing throughout most of the world, gradually evolving into different species. But during that two million years, they never advanced in skills or lifestyle beyond the Stone Age level.

Yuval Noah Harari asks the $64,000 question: "What then drove forward the evolution of the massive human brain during those two million years?" and answers, "Frankly, we don't know."[7] It had not been a gradual evolution—the archaic humans never gained any significant advances over those two million years. The change was sudden and huge and, once it happened, by 70,000 years ago, Homo sapiens left Africa, passed to the Middle East, then moved on throughout the world.

HOW HOMO SAPIENS CONQUERED THE WORLD

Over the years we have experienced a few superficial genetic changes, such as skin color, height, and eye color, but little evolutionary modification, and we all still share roughly the same mental and physical abilities.[8] The biggest change has been cultural, where some people learned how to *write* down their thoughts and observations, and with that written record they began the *accumulation* of a body of knowledge. With those two great assets, the physical sciences gradually developed, leading to all the technical advances we see today.

As they spread throughout the world modern men and women encountered the many primitive members of the Homo genus. DNA science has shown that the current world population carries a 1–6 percent set of genes from a few of those archaic species, including the Neanderthals and Denisovans.[9] However, all those archaic humans had disappeared by 10,000 years ago. Harari suggests that it was no coincidence that when sapiens arrived in a new locale, the local populations disappeared shortly thereafter. "It's our current exclusivity, not that multi-species past, that is peculiar—and perhaps incriminating… it may well have been the first and most significant ethnic-cleansing campaign in history…we Sapiens have good reasons to repress the memory of our siblings."[10]

That condemnation is a little exaggerated, perhaps, because the sapiens species had by 50,000 years ago become more differentiated from the archaic species than when they first appeared. After that, cross-species breeding became unlikely. Tolerance has never been a key feature of modern man, and the archaic people may have appeared no different than all the lesser animals that inhabited the earth as the Sapiens began to exert their unique cranial muscles.

HUNTER-GATHERERS ADVANCE THEIR SKILLS

Between their origin, somewhere from 150,000 years ago up to 70,000 years ago, our direct sapiens ancestors accomplished little at first, but when they burst out of Africa, they spread around the Asian continent in short order, reaching Australia about 30,000 years ago and crossed into the American continents about 20,000 years ago. In the period from 70,000 to 40,000 years ago they developed a greater capacity for speech; invented boats, oil lamps, bows and arrows, and needles; produced art; engaged in commerce; and honored religious beliefs.[11] Those examples of cognitive thinking and new linguistic skills represent the Cognitive Revolution that propelled sapiens far ahead of the archaic humans.

Yuval Harari points to the new supple and abstract mental abilities of these humans as enabling them to comprehend fictions, compared to merely stating facts. It is one thing to communicate—"there is a lion on that path"—but most impressive to organize a community, select a leader, warn another not to trust another, trade goods, abide by laws, and understand the meaning of justice. "Ever since the Cognitive Revolution, Sapiens has thus been living in a dual reality. On the one hand, the objective reality of rivers, trees and lions; and on the other hand, the imagined reality of gods, nations, and corporations."[12]

The unique nature of speech and all the related cranial and biological accessories necessary for its usage has been described in detail by Merlin Donald: "One thing is certain: if we compare the complex architecture of the modern mind with that of an ape, we must conclude that the Darwinian universe is too small to contain humanity. We are a different order…. Our minds function on several…perceptual planes, none of which are available to animals…. Theories of human evolution must be expanded, modified to accommodate all possibilities."[13]

Professor Donald's analysis reveals that regardless of their origins, Homo sapiens were revolutionary beings. They moved fast and far: Starting as Stone Age "cavemen," imaginative individuals—think Fred Flintstone and Barney Rubble—invented rollers, and then the wheel, kickstarting the beginning of the Industrial Revolution. Later people developed levers, pulleys, and geared windmills. Progress advanced continuously—less than 10,000 years ago people created alphabets, recorded their thoughts in books, and investigated the laws of physical science. In just the last few centuries, continued advances unraveled the mystery of atoms, chemicals, and supersonic flight.

All that was done by people, individuals, and teams of individuals. One thing does appear certain: those people must be credited with all human progress. They literally picked themselves up by their own bootstraps! There—the most politically incorrect line ever! But face it—who else did all that? The rivers? The historians? The governments? The trees?

It has been fashionable lately to assert that human progress was determined by the climate and geography of their settlements, but the fact that Homo sapiens traveled from Africa to the entire surface of the globe makes one wonder: Why did some make such a poor choice as to settle and remain in unfavorable locales? It was mankind's first colonization of the planet and they had the opportunity to pick any spot they wanted. Naturally, the groups that avoided the worst swamps, jungles, and deserts, and avoided isolated locales, fared the best and slowly accumulated social and technical knowledge that allowed higher levels of living.

Then, about 15,000 years ago, the last ice age gave way during a period of global warming. The glaciers retreated toward the two poles. The warmer climate was ideal for farming, some people adopted a more settled way of life, and by 7000 BC there were the beginnings of large urban communities. The Middle East, Africa, and Asia were peppered with permanent villages, with their people laboring in their fields, introducing new and better ways to produce food. The more food they produced, the faster the populations grew, as did the corresponding need for a governing elite, an element of government that has tended to both lead and oppress most of the world's people to this day. Ever since that new sedentary lifestyle began, "we have revved up the treadmill of life to ten times its former speed and made our days more anxious and agitated."[14]

THE AGRICULTURAL REVOLUTION AND THE NEED FOR ELITES

The transition from hunting to farming was slow, but by 7,000 years ago, many human societies had moved from the hunter-gathering status to full-time farming and begun the domestication of animals to provide milk, meat, and use them as beasts of burden. These changes have been widely touted as wonderful progress for mankind but, like most change, the results for human communities were both good and bad!

As hunter-gatherers, our ancestors had roamed the earth for over 75,000 years and were rarely, if ever, burdened by elites. They didn't need them. They lived in small family groups and the senior members cared for their kinfolk, so all went reasonably well. There was no need for government, taxes, or regulations. But then some groups decided to take up agriculture, herding animals, and tilling the soil. Settled communities then developed independently in numerous areas of the world—wherever there were wild grains and beasts of burden to domesticate. Douglas Preston has found evidence even in the deepest jungles of Central America, where the people found ways to clear land for gardens and to add charcoal and ashes from their fires to make the soil more fertile and productive.[15]

Agricultural practices then spread so that by the first century AD most people throughout the world were growing their own food. In a few isolated locations where that didn't occur, the people remained in a hunter-gatherer Stone Age culture where time stood still. During just the last 150 years, explorers have discovered their descendants still living as freely and happily as they always have in isolated areas such as New Guinea, the Darien Zone of Panama, islands in the South Pacific, the Australian Outback, the Amazon jungle, and sub-Saharan Africa.

But for most communities, growing their own crops made sense: "If you worked harder, you would have a better life. That was the plan."[16] It may well have been the first time we followed our community organizers' advice, never suspecting the advice was slyly slanted to give them the better life, and ourselves a life of subservience, forever feeding those at the top. Regardless of the pros and cons, what happened made big changes in human destiny:

First, the number of people increased rapidly with all that food.

Second, most everyone became doomed forever to toil in the fields 24/7 to tend to the plants and animals.

Third, there was a need for a chosen few to manage all the new complexity of counting, storing, and distributing the vast foodstuffs that the workers were able to produce.

Fourth, with many people living close together, "they needed more effective ways of resolving conflict and more elaborate notions of property."[17]

And that is how it all came to pass: Voila! The elites, experts, tax collectors, and bureaucrats were born—new social groups that would supervise the workers and fare quite well ever after, without getting their hands dirty!

In *Sapiens*, the author describes those extraordinary developments: "Hunter-gatherers spent their time in more stimulating and varied ways and were less in danger of starvation and disease. The Agricultural Revolution certainly enlarged the sum total of food at the disposal of humankind, but the extra food did not translate into a better diet or more leisure. Rather, it translated into population explosions and pampered elites…the Agricultural Revolution was history's biggest fraud."[18]

THE EMERGENCE OF EMPIRES

The spread of Homo sapiens around the world was never gentle on their environment: Wherever they appeared throughout the world they managed to drive other living things to extinction. During the period leading up to the Agricultural Age, from 50,000 to 10,000 years ago, one-half of the world's large mammalian species, along with all the species of archaic humans, disappeared. Yuval Harari writes that this "first wave of Sapiens colonization was one of the biggest and swiftest ecological disasters to befall the animal kingdom."[19]

It may be instructive to acknowledge that every human being living today has ancestors who despoiled the environment, drove entire species of animal life to extinction, and participated in the genocide of all archaic human beings. And, in the process, the members of every race and nationality throughout history employed slaves, concubines, eunuchs, serfs, and peasants to obey their bidding. The good news is that we have ended most of that oppression in the last couple hundred years by advancing freedom as an end in itself—the biggest obstacle being the elites in countries that still engage in those unjust and oppressive practices.

Homo sapiens committed a second wave of extinction between 10,000 and 3,000 BC as a result of taking up farming and the transition to settled communities. Harari writes, "Don't believe the tree huggers who claim that our ancestors lived in harmony with nature. Long before the Industrial Revolution, Homo sapiens held the record among all organisms for driving the most plant and animal species to their extinction."[20] And, sadly, that destruction will probably continue as long as the human population keeps increasing.

As history marched onward, elites moved up the social scale, allowed their record-keepers and overseers to form a middle layer above the workers, and thereby gained both leisure and total luxury for themselves. Then, as large communities became civilizations, such as in the Egyptian, Chinese, and Assyrian empires of 3000 BC, the ruling elites supported a priestly class to provide spiritual cohesion and reassurance to their people. Those elites may have been the first to utilize fantastic ceremonial rituals as an "opium for the masses."

The change to modernity has not been all bad. The 4,000-year period of our earliest recorded history, 3000 BC–1000 AD, displayed the fruits of the Agricultural Age and witnessed the rise of advanced nation states, art, sculpture, books, and the beginnings of medical and physical sciences, all of which made life richer and more meaningful for Homo sapiens. Dozens of large civilizations formed throughout the world centered on large urban centers, with formal religions, some form of writing, administrative laws, and the beginnings of mathematical advances, literature, and political experiments.

So, is the backbreaking work required worth it all?! It would be if we could just get the same practical people to manage our governments that created our modern medicines, efficient business enterprises, and advanced technologies. That would require gaining a better control over those who we let manage our governments. Their major failings in governance currently appear to be corruption for self-gain and the use of abstract theories to convince us that they know how to change everything for the better. However, those are two very major failings when you consider that their real job is to just run the government efficiently, equitably, and honestly!

SUMMARY

There are four problems that all people on earth have always faced when they designed and administered their communities: First, ever since the Agricultural Revolution, there have always been elites, and there always will be. Second, there is a bit of larceny in almost every heart so it is essential to limit the ruling elite's greed. Third, even in democracies, freedom will always be limited to a degree by the need for safety and order. Fourth, there can never be a workable egalitarian or totally just society until all people are saints. (Don't hold your breath for that last one!)

In short, our freedom will always be limited, the elites self-serving, and we will never attain equality of results for all people. The solution is to make sure that each limit placed on our freedom is truly necessary, that the greed of leaders is monitored and minimized, and that the differences in wealth and incomes never become so large and sustained that they destroy the unity and morale of the people. Entering into any social compact requires many concessions. If we are to live together and enjoy the blessings of freedom there will of necessity be some bumps in the road, but accepting tyranny, waste, and gross injustice should not be among them.

In most Western democracies today, there are too many limits on personal freedom, not enough limits on corruption among elites, and unconscionable differences in wealth. Whatever the reason, these are three big problems, and our future may depend on fixing them. In the next chapter we will look at how those problems have impacted all people and how only a few dealt with them successfully.

CHAPTER 2-

How Elites Gain Their Privileged Position

Governments live off their citizens so…they are inevitably parasites. By taking over functions which used to be a matter for society, however, they become something more like a malignant tumor.
Ivo Mosley: In the Name of the People, 123

THE INDEPENDENT GROWTH OF AGRICULTURAL communities created a variety of elites who were needed to oversee the administration of these increasingly complex societies. Those leadership positions were usually grasped by the most ambitious and ingenious individuals who preferred to supervise the workers rather than participate in the work. To gain those supervisory positions they often claimed to possess special powers, used myths and arcane knowledge to justify their rule, and used raw power when needed to neutralize doubters. And they also work to divide the people into warring groups to avoid any combined opposition to their rule.

By creating a stratification of social classes, they pit the middle classes against the lower classes, one race against another, vilify the corporations, set urban dwellers against rural, rich against poor, and victims against victors, In fact, it has been the elites who have been the real victors. The results have been unfortunate: Almost all the world's people have lived under stultifying oppression for the last 5,000 years—a very long time, especially if you have been among the oppressed!

Nothing illustrates the cruel and selfish methods of most rulers and exposes their determination to live off the labor of others than their historic readiness to subject fellow human beings to a life of slavery. Since the earliest agricultural communities, more than five thousand years ago, elites have used slaves to perform the laborious tasks that they didn't want to dirty their hands with. The people of every ethnicity on earth have conscripted such forced labor wherever they were able to subdue other humans and chain them to a lifetime of service. For example, after the sea battle of Lepanto in 1571 the Venetian and Spanish victors freed 15,000 Christian galley slaves from the defeated Turk-Muslim fleet.

Slavery was so pernicious that even in the earliest democratic republics, where personal liberty was extended to large portions of their community, there were still large numbers held as slaves. Note that slaves were owned by elites. Most of the "whites" that are blamed as a group for past slavery laws are still barely keeping their heads above water. Gaining freedom from a ruling class has been a long slow and very gradual slog for all humankind!

Thousands of years ago, as revealed in the Old Testament, we discover the eternal and uncaring attitude of elites:

When the Lord asked Cain, "Where is your brother Abel?" Cain replied, "I don't know. Am I my brother's keeper?"

GENESIS 4:9

All we have to do is look back to a small Pennsylvania town on November 18, 1863, to see how difficult it has been to overcome such oppression. That was the day that a rough-cut American president, a man who began his working career in the backwoods of Kentucky as a rail-splitter, was scheduled to give one of his few major speeches. Lee Habeeb has described the scene: "He was visiting the town, with a population of less than 3,000, but nearly 15,000 people would gather the next day to dedicate a new Soldiers' National Cemetery."[21] The small town was named Gettysburg and it had just witnessed one of the bloodiest and most decisive battles of the Civil War, a brutal battle, with over 50,000 casualties.

President "Abe" Lincoln spoke briefly, after what could have been, "the real Gettysburg address," delivered by the former US Senator and Harvard College President Edward Everett, which, as Habeeb writes, "went on and on for nearly two hours, but has been long forgotten."[22] Then, when the former rail-splitter took the podium, he spoke just 269 words. The speech lasted less than two minutes, but Lincoln made it clear that the intentions of America's Founding Fathers and the reason for the Civil War were the same: to form a nation dedicated to the proposition that all men are created equal and each person is entitled to equal respect and rights. That "great experiment," the work of many Americans, was not a neat or tidy process; it had taken centuries to extend freedom to all citizens and is still a work in progress. But the basic principles involved had been firmly established over the past few thousand years.

HOW ELITES ADAPT THEIR TYRANNICAL METHODS

In more modern times, without slaves, and being increasingly subjected to watchful voters, the elites have had to resort to more sophisticated methods. Douglas Preston refers to the primitive civilizations in Central America that existed 500–1,500 years ago where "those noble lords with access to the 'ultimate truths' leveraged that knowledge to control the masses, avoid physical labor, and amass wealth for themselves."[23] Preston goes on to explain that in America today this continues not only in religious cults "but also in the quasi-religious practice of capitalism: specifically in extremely high CEO compensation (necessary because of esoteric knowledge), and on Wall Street, where bankers dismiss criticism by claiming that the common people do not understand the complex, important, and multilayered financial transactions they are engaged in as they do 'God's work'—to quote the CEO of Goldman Sachs."[24]

Nowhere is that nonsense about having special knowledge spewed more freely than by the practitioners of "economics" who claim to know how to manage the economy, to promote growth, avoid depressions, provide jobs, improve the schools, stimulate the economy, help the poor, punish evil industries, improve the environment, etc. Having listened to those claims for the past seventy years since WWII, I can attest that poverty has not decreased, unemployment figures have not improved, and inequality of income and wealth has gotten worse.

All the elites need to do currently is get the politicians to twist the rules and regulations so that they get advantages, and their citizens get burdened with obstacles. Elites do not want us to gain wealth, have the right to bear arms or free speech, to worship the Faith of our choosing, or to see one standard of justice uniformly applied to all. We may not know it, but we are all gradually becoming slaves once again.

There is a saying among politicians that they "should never let a crisis go to waste." They understand that in times of crisis the voters will look to them for a solution, and then they will be able to expand government and thereby increase their own power. Looking at America today, in 2021, it appears that the elites may be deliberately creating crises. Why else would they be hyping the Corona virus, closing the schools and stores, running up trillions of dollars in debt, distributing

money so people will not need to work, financing Chinese germ war-
fare laboratories, making everyone wear masks, and creating a crisis
at our borders?

It certainly makes no sense to make us wear masks to go in a
store yet allow untested immigrants to enter and spread around the
countryside without masks. And it surely makes no sense to require
identification to get a vaccine or a hunting license but not to vote. It
seems unbelievable, but could it be that creating problems, virtual sabotage, has become their newest way to adapt their tyrannical methods
of controlling the people.

WHO ARE THE ELITES?

Many writers have tried to describe the powerful cliques that
dictate much of American policy, often referring to them as a "Blob"
because they are a shadowy and changing assortment. Allies of the
elites dismiss such opinions as mere "conspiracy theories" in an effort
to hide the selfish nature of such amorphous forces. However, Professor
G. William Domhoff has done a very good job of identifying who
makes up the inner power in our ruling elites and does so in such
scholarly detail that the possibility of it being just a conspiracy theory
becomes absurd.[25]

His subtitle does, however, confuse the true message of his
book–*The Triumph of the Corporate Rich*–probably makes many readers and reviewers conclude that corporations are the danger, which is
not the real lesson we learn from that book. On page 106 the author
provides a diagram that shows the three-part network of special interests that collaborate in determining America's direction. One part is
made up of the social elites and jetsetters, bonded by common prep
school ties and social club festivities. Another segment is made up
of corporate executives and directors who wield social and lobbying power over other members of the ruling elite. The third group is

the planning and advisory community composed of hired experts, academics, economists, and the directors of think tanks and many supposedly charitable foundations.

Members of those three groups are all united by the fact that they belong to an upper-class social society and wield influence from their lofty positions as directors, executives, and trustees of powerful institutions. The actual politicians holding office can arise from anywhere but most of them soon adopt the canons of the elites who finance their campaigns and invite them to join their social activities. The evidence that Domhoff presents reveals "the high level of class dominance in the United States."[26] The fact that members of all three groups meet socially in their fashionable clubs, parties, and collegiate environments illustrates how their ideas on government policy become unified among themselves while they remain both oblivious and unconcerned about the vast public beneath them.

During the last 40 years the firm control exerted by these individuals is demonstrated by how politicians running for office no longer kiss babies at campaign stops but quite differently consider both the babies and their parents to be deplorable denizens of fly-over country still clinging to their guns and faith. They have even uttered such opinions in public!

Because of the economic mobility still existing in America's primarily capitalist economy, there are many new members of the financial and corporate elites who are rising to high offices from lower socio-economic classes. However, they usually become co-opted by the social circles where they can now gain entrance. Their outlook soon becomes shaped anew by their new glamorous associates. It is easy to understand that any "outsider" would have to bend his beliefs and principles a great deal to gain acceptance into such a corrupt and self-centered group. Much as they talk about diversity, the elites today admit no contrarians to their inner circle.

Although descriptions of "elites" may be interesting, they do not matter for our purposes. The ruling elites, whoever they may be, have always posed a threat to free people. The important factor is that they must be controlled by the people—otherwise they will assume excess power, embrace the temptations of corrupt practices, and get to believe they are superior to the common men and women of their country. They may even start dictating what is appropriate speech and behavior to their citizens, and thus stamp out the freedom they are supposed to protect!

THE HUMAN NEED FOR SECURITY AND COMFORT

It is commonly understood that most claims of competency can be taken with a big skeptical grain of salt, for the predictions of experts have proven almost always to be wildly incorrect. And yet most humans seem to have a strong need for some certainty about the future. America's elites know this and happily provide predictions of looming problems and tout their ability to save us.

Scott Armstrong, an expert in forecasting at the Wharton School, explains this irrational desire with his seersucker theory: "No matter how much evidence exists that seers do not exist, suckers will pay for the existence of seers."[27]

Dan Gardner has written a book on this same subject to "explain why expert predictions fail and why we believe them anyway." He points out the obvious fact that the nature of reality and the behavior of human beings is so complex that the future cannot be predicted. "Try to predict an unpredictable world using an error prone brain and you get the gaffes that litter history."[28]

Nevertheless, many of us believe those who offer us predictions because our brains are hardwired with an aversion to uncertainty. Our ancestors' survival relied on some knowledge of potential danger so their brains evolved with a need to know, for with a little advance warning they might just escape some very bad events.

Gardner's book *Future Babble* suggests that there are two types of minds: Foxes and Hedgehogs. The latter are often seen as experts, confident of their conclusions, articulate, convincing, authoritative, and often wrong but never in doubt. They are found among newspaper columnists, talking heads, media superstars, lecturers, political celebrities, and experts on pundit panels, bestseller lists, and lecture circuits. Foxes are more cautious, ready to change their opinions as needed, and rarely invited on talk shows.

The destructive role of elites was the subject of a recent book by Angelo M. Codevilla, in which he indicates that "The Ruling Class' chief pretension is its intellectual superiority: its members claim to know things that the common herd cannot."[29] Sadly, many voters accept their advice and believe the politicians' promises to make things better. However, the fact is that the elites live off the work of that common herd; their careers depend on huge financial corporations and big government; most would be unemployable if there were no such comfy havens offering them employment.

Thus, the Ruling Class, as members of their nation's establishment, are truly parasites, living off the institutions that pay them and the gullibility of many voters who support them. The irony is that the elite's predictions and warnings have rarely helped any of us: their predictions have usually proven incorrect and their warnings too late.

THE PERSISTENCE OF ELITE DOMINANCE

Even the nations usually considered to be republics or democracies have eventually been ruled by an elite group that found a way to accumulate the wealth, prestige, and political clout to dominate their government. It is not just in the dictatorships that elites have imposed their will on the people; it has happened in every settled society forever.

Elites have almost always wanted a larger than average share of the pie and have no problem with the people below them getting less.

The accompanying chart shows the share of total income received by the five separate income quintiles of the American households for the last 50 years. It demonstrates that the percentage share of the bottom three quintiles has never increased but has gone down by 20–26 percent during that period. The second from the top has declined by about 8 percent. Quite differently, the top quintile's share has increased 22 percent!

Thus, only the top quintile got more of the pie and everyone else got less. That did not happen by chance. The elites in our capitols have made thousands of "adjustments" over those fifty years so that the laws, taxes, and regulations will help them. They have never liked Abraham Lincoln's line about "a government by the people and for the people."

Jeffrey A. Winters, in his comprehensive review of oligarchies, explained their ubiquity: "Regardless of political context or historical period, oligarchs are defined consistently as actors who claim or own concentrated personal wealth and are empowered by it. They are a social and political by-product of extreme material stratification in societies."[30]

SHARE OF HOUSEHOLD INCOME (%)

	Bottom 5th	2nd 5th	3rd 5th	4th 5th	Top 5th
2018	3.1	8.3	14.1	22.6	52.0
2008	3.4	8.6	14.7	23.3	50.0
1998	3.6	9.0	15.0	23.2	49.2
1988	3.8	9.6	16.0	24.2	46.3
1978	4.2	10.2	16.8	24.7	44.1
1968	4.2	11.1	17.6	24.5	42.6
Change	-1.1	-2.8	-3.5	-1.9	+9.4
% change	-26%	-25%	-20%	-8.0%	+22%

U. S. Bureau of the Census Annual Social and Economic Supplements

Recent extreme examples of this distorted influence from elites were seen when Mayor Bloomberg pledged to contribute tens of millions of dollars in key swing states to elect Democratic politicians, and how such billionaires as the Koch brothers and George Soros spent huge amounts of cash to favor their personal partisan objectives. Winters tells us that "Building a democracy and taming oligarchs through laws—two quite different achievements—are vital first steps along the path...for addressing the extreme injustices of wealth."[31]

Winters also points out, "There is nothing automatic about ending oligarchy through the adoption of free and participatory forms of government... ending oligarchy is impossible unless the power resource that defines oligarchs—concentrated wealth—is dispersed. This has happened many times in history as a consequence of war, conquest, or revolution. However, it has never been successfully attempted as a democratic decision."[32]

Winters calls for a "taming of oligarchs" but concedes that it is not an easy task, that taming oligarchs through laws does not eliminate them, but that doing so "is better than allowing the societal hardship and pathologies of wild oligarchs to continue unchecked."[33] His suggestion is to reduce the "oligarchic intensity" and thereby address the injustices of having an extremely overpowering elite control the direction of a nation's destiny. Recent attempts to censor opinion by such giant corporations as Facebook and Google illustrate the oligarchic intensity that we face in America.

However, a free economy will result in some people gaining great wealth, and that can be good for the nation. Individuals are motivated by a big payoff. Egalitarians have some valid points, but a nation cannot kill the geese that lay golden eggs. Good institutions must allow fortunes to be made by the innovators who make better things for better living and create the jobs that employ most citizens. But there is a limit to how much that fortune needs to be. The recent dot-com billionaires may well have gone over such limits. We see again that nothing about people is ever simply black or white; it's all about the relative degree of liberty, power, and oppression.

TWISTING THE LAWS TO GAIN SPECIAL ADVANTAGES

In this book there are many references to how elites manage to tweak the laws and institutions to benefit themselves. That is how they gain an edge over the people. Getting Congress to create "loopholes" in tax laws has been one way they do that. More recently, they bene-fitted from the Supreme Court's quirky decision that corporations are "people" and thus allowed under the Constitution to enjoy free speech. Now, the Bill of Rights is generally interpreted as a means to guarantee each citizen an equal voice in government and an equal opportunity to participate. The right to free speech thus ensures that each person is free to support issues and candidates with their spoken or written words; the question became whether that right extends to corporations and does free speech include the giving of money?

The Supreme Court justices somehow decided that giving money is a form of free speech and the elites thus gained the right for a wealthy person to contribute, either directly or through PACs and corporations, vast sums to a political candidate of their liking. Thus, a thousand common people will henceforth never be able to "speak" as much as a single billionaire who is able to contribute heavily to a polit-ical candidate. That court decision gave the wealthy a bigger "voice" and, consequently a greater role in the country's future than the average citizen—and that is a perfect example of how elites gain control. The legendary cowboy Will Rogers once boasted that "America has the best government money can buy," and that remains even more true today.

Reducing inequality was "supposedly" attempted when just thirty-five years ago, the top inheritance tax was at 70 percent. The devil in the details was that the IRS Code had many loopholes in the form of trusts and gifting that allowed the very rich to avoid that top tax bracket for a few generations. And all the talk about raising income taxes on the wealthiest individuals will not end their oligarchic standing. There is a reason why our children are not taught personal finance: The elites don't want them to understand that the very rich, those with 50 million or more, are virtually immune to income taxes. Forget the 2.5% income, or $1,250,000 annually, that 50 million dollars can earn when invested. The big deal is the investments themselves; invested well, they will normally increase in value by at least 4–6 percent, or between two and three million dollars every year. The very rich could pay 100% tax on their income, but by selling a couple million dollars of their appreciated investments, and paying a low capital gains tax, end up with a few million dollars of spending money each year—and their net worth would still keep increasing.

That simple fact is never mentioned when we debate the level of income tax. That debate, however, does distract from the more significant issue of wealth and capital gains taxes. Thus, when the elites argue over taxes on the wealthy, they often bring out the smoke and mirrors, like the magicians they emulate, and do the opposite of what they appear to do. What can the average voter do? It has become a full-time job to keep up with the elite's deceptions, and the once fabled "muck-raking" media no longer help sort out all the chicanery in Washington.

THE DIFFERENCE BETWEEN "SOFT" AND "HARD" SCIENTISTS

Just as the common people come in many varieties, so do elites. There is actually a need for some types of elites—scientists like Jonas

Salk who eliminated polio, geniuses like Mozart and Johnny Cash who created great music, artists like Van Gogh who gave us Impressionist masterpieces, and those like Edison, Colt, Deere, Faraday, Edison, and Einstein who gave us great innovative technologies and advanced the modern scientific method. Add the bright engineers and mechanics, chemists, and doctors, who developed technologies and medicines that helped mankind. Those are the "hard," or physical creative scientists, and they have been a blessing that keeps on giving. You can identify them easily: If they make an actual product or provide a useful service, they are valuable members of any community.

Groucho Marx: Politicians and elites were grist for his humor, the butt of his jokes

But did we really need those "soft scientists" like Hegel, who contributed to the idea that a master race should rule and crush inferior beings? Or academics like President Woodrow Wilson who got us into WWI, and gave us the Federal Reserve Bank, the League of Nations, and the IRS. Or economic theorists like Karl Marx who outlined the type of government that Lenin and Stalin used to enslave and murder millions of their countrymen and women? Those are the "experts" who produce no tangible or beneficial product—just ideas, theories, and suggestions that may or may not work. Thomas Sowell refers to them as merely "dealers in second-hand ideas."

The problem with those soft scientists is that a majority have been full-time professional politicians, consultants, or academics with little experience in the real world of business. They have never learned how to make anything, provide any kind of services, or how to cooperate and work with people. Quite the opposite: our experts and elected officials' experience is largely shaped by mastering the art of giving speeches, raising funds, getting elected, and holding onto their office once elected. Sadly, none of that provides the useful experience needed to perform their elected duties.

The elected officials in Congress do not even appear to know what their duties are: that they are supposed to make sure the American government, the largest organization in the world, is run efficiently and honestly. Instead, they concentrate on changing everything, trying to solve unsolvable problems, spending our money, and wasting time fighting over partisan and theoretical issues. "We do not need 'change' as much as the competent administration of existing laws…. If there is to be a beneficial 'transformation' of our government, it should come from competent and honest management more than from creating loopholes for themselves or chasing utopian dreams."[34]

In brief, most of our elites are inexperienced, selfish, corrupt, and/or passionately partisan and ideological. Not for nothing do they enjoy the lowest popularity rating of every American group other than convicted murderers. There are exceptions, many of them, but not enough to buck the tide of the majority. As Tucker Carlson writes,

"America now has not only one of the least impressive ruling classes in history, but also the least self-aware. They have no idea how bad they are."[35]

ARE OUR ELITES GETTING OVER-CONFIDENT?

The ruling elites seemed in 2016 to be destined to elect the Clintons back into the White House following Barack Obama's presidency. That would have resulted in thirty-six consecutive years of Bush-Clinton-Bush-Obama-Clinton presidencies. Perhaps the elites had reason to be over-confident, certain that they had taken over from what they saw as a hide-bound antiquated culture with masses of ignorant citizens.

FAMOUS LAST WORDS

..."to be just grossly generalistic, you could put half of Trump's supporters into what I call the 'basket of deplorables.'"

HILLARY CLINTON, SEPTEMBER 9, 2016

In the past, especially in democracies like America where everyone can vote, the elites were careful to project a deep respect and even love of their fellow countrymen and women. Times have changed. When President Obama referred to Mid-westerners as those "who still cling to their guns and faith," and Romney wrote off 47 percent of the voters, and Hillary Clinton went a step further by simply insulting them as "deplorables," the class divide became too big to miss. A purely power-hungry elite would never have made such a blunder. But America's elites have gone beyond their purely selfish roots. They have come to believe they are superior to the common people. As Angelo Codevilla writes,

"The class's chief pretension is its intellectual superiority; its members claim to know things that the common herd cannot."[36]

Recently, that arrogance caught the attention of many voters in a way that the details of policy could never gain. In 2016 there was an upwelling of anti-Hillary voters coming out of the fields and factories to voice their dislike of her, her husband, and her opinions. The voters had woken up to the fact that the elites, the media, and the academics were all lined up against them.

The smarmy, polished voices of the Washington establishment, both Democrats and Republicans, did not ring true. Their obvious corruption proved to be their undoing. The elites had asked for it, by insulting the intelligence and habits of the common people. They had woken a sleeping giant that roared. Tucker Carlson called it a "howl of rage."

SUMMARY

The biggest danger posed by today's elites is that they have changed dramatically for the worse compared to the elites of antiquity. Our current elites' strategy has been to promote political correctness as a religion and have the schools and colleges indoctrinate our youth to believe in the "progressive" mantra that government should solve all their problems. They want us to live in the moment, on credit, obedient to their goals, never resistant, never critical, ever hopeful. It is arguable that it would make more sense for us to rely on God's Grace than on the promises of our elites. He may not intervene very often to help us, but at least He does not stay up nights plotting how to hurt us!

Always remember that the elites produce no tangible items that help maintain a growing economy. Instead, they allow massive waste of the taxpayers' money, engage in endless foreign military escapades, argue over abstract theories, pile up massive debt, and engage in constant nefarious financial and legal chicanery to enrich themselves, their relatives, and their friends. Little has changed in human governance over the last 3,700 years since Hammurabi ruled in Babylon and made his people build his palace and its spectacular hanging gardens---except the extraordinary rise of a few rare democratic societies. Those great discoveries of mankind, where ordinary people were able to create "start-up" nations, and escape for a time the burden of elites, are the subject of the next chapter.

CHAPTER 3-

"Start-Up Nations"–How Avoiding Elites Allowed Freedom

 *"The preservation of freedom is the protective reason for limiting and decentralizing governmental power. But there is also a constructive reason. The great advances of civilization, whether in architecture, or painting, in science or literature, in industry or agriculture, have never come from centralized government."*
—Milton Friedman, Capitalism and Freedom

FRIEDMAN CLEARLY IS AMONG THOSE who support a free and open business environment, without excessive government regulation, because, in his opinion, the great advances of civilization have never come from governments. Government officials, like referees, are not supposed to score touchdowns; their function is simply to maintain an open and free economy with opportunity for everyone else to score their own victories.

One of the best ways to evaluate Friedman's comment is to look at history's "start-up" nations where a group of ordinary people settled a new land and succeeded for centuries without any large government or class of experts, academics, or elites. Those case studies, which describe some of the most successful societies in history, suggest that we do not need a big government when it comes to building a thriving free and prosperous community. All that needs doing is to encourage a positive contribution from everyone in the population.

That does not mean that every citizen is an exemplary contributor to their community, but that out of many there emerges a large number who contribute significantly. Because humans are complex beings, and their future achievements are never readily predictable, it is vital to offer every child the opportunity to develop to his or her fullest potential and in that way to gain a positive effort from a maximum number of people.

The people of Judea, Phoenicia, and Greece were among the earliest creators of liberty and widespread opportunities. Their good fortune was to find a new and often harsh locale where they could escape invasion by neighboring nations intent on pillage and conquest. For the Israelites, who were surrounded by enemies, the secret was a cultural and religious solidarity so firm that it outlasted all conquests.

In their sanctuaries, the Phoenician and ancient Greek people established the balance between enough but not too much government. Their unusual freedom was based on their fresh start, with an energetic and enterprising group, willing to endure hardship to gain liberty and opportunity.

Those rustic settlements were shaped by their primitive character which imposed an egalitarian nature on their inhabitants. Their success, and those who followed their example, in multiple locales and times, provides evidence that it was the common people who built successful nations.

THE LABORATORIES OF HISTORY

Jean-Francois Revel has described those rare times in history when what we might call "good governance" appeared.[37] The ancient Greeks were one of the first to give a voice to a large portion of their people. The resulting glory of their achievements has stood as a landmark to all who followed. They were preceded by the Phoenicians, a merchant-based trading society that enjoyed unusual equality and prosperity.

Those rare cases demonstrated what free and united people could do: it's all about having personal and economic freedom, and only a little oppression. The Phoenicians had seized that type of opportunity on the edge of the Mediterranean Sea. There, they were overlooked by the huge autocratic nations inland—the conflicts between Egypt and the Babylonian empires passed them by across the inland areas of Judea and the Tigris Valley.

THE "STEPPING STONES" OF HISTORY

"In each period that is marked by historical progress, there exists what one might call a "laboratory society" where civilization's great inventions are tested.

JEAN-FRANCOIS REVEL *ANTI-AMERICANISM*

Left to their own devices, the Phoenicians succeeded, with little in the way of natural resources or arable land. They did it by building ships and developing extensive trading routes throughout the Mediterranean Sea. Their civilization survived for a thousand years before Alexander the Great found a way to build a causeway to their island homes and burn everything to the ground. It is hard to blame them for this eventual defeat for young Alexander was not dubbed "the Great" for nothing—he was tutored by Aristotle until the age of sixteen, became King of Macedonia at age twenty in 336 BC, and within thirteen years proceeded to conquer almost every nation everywhere, from the westernmost settlements in the Mediterranean world across the Middle East to the Indus Valley.

The Phoenician contribution to posterity was to demonstrate that a free merchant class enjoying roughly equal status could prosper despite poor geography and few natural resources. And they settled another large democratic state in North Africa, Carthage, which followed in their footsteps until foreign overreach by their leaders weakened their power. Their leaders chose to send Hannibal with an army of elephants, across the Mediterranean Sea, through Spain and France, then over the Alps, and down into Italy to sack Rome—a decision that makes America's escapade in Vietnam almost seem sensible!

In reprise, Roman legions sacked Carthage, burning the entire city to the ground. The Carthaginians' terrible demise offers a stark reminder to people everywhere—if you let your nation weaken, or become divided or overextended, you invite the risk of being invaded, despoiled, and enslaved. Never forget that in just the last eighty-five years, almost every nation in Asia, Europe, and Africa has been violently invaded and occupied due to the incompetence of their elites or the greed of the elites in control of the invading armies. Note, it has never been the common people of nations who started those wars or invasions. That's what elites do. And, naturally, they stay way behind the fighting front lines.

The important thing about the Phoenicians is that they left an indelible mark on all future civilizations, settling Portugal, introducing manufacturing processes to supplement their trade, and illustrating that a large community of businessmen/traders could work together without a burdensome administrative state or an intellectual class regulating their activities.

ANCIENT GREECE AND ROME

The Greeks and Romans filled the vacuum left by the Phoenicians as democratic republics and lords of the Mediterranean world. They were among the most successful start-up nations in history. Victor Davis Hanson has told the story of the early Greeks, the rural Hoplites, and that their history from 700–300 BC, the polis period, "is understandable only through appreciation of the presence of an automatous group of independent farmers."[38]

Because they were free and owned their land and homes, those farmers were always ready, willing, and able to pick up arms and defend their turf against all invaders. "These agrarians were most definitely not peasants, but rather had title to their small farms, enjoyed political rights as full citizens…and were responsible for the general Greek cultural characteristics of pragmatism, confidence in the middling classes, individualism, and self-reliance—a new ideology that appeared as early as Hesiod and the lyric poets."[39]

By 800 BC they had established a culture that featured not only the pride and humanism of ancient Greece but also the inquisitive and scientific mind of their earliest philosopher-scientist, Hesiod. Victor Davis Hanson has pointed out the unique nature of these early Greeks: "There was really no word in the Egyptian, Persian, or Assyrian language for 'constitution,' 'freedom,' 'citizen,' 'politics,' 'or 'polis'—the essence of Western civilization that began in the Greek countryside somewhere in the eighth century B. C."[40] In effect these rural farmers not only created the mechanics and ideas that established individual freedom but they also carved out new words required to capture the essence of those great discoveries.

The Greek people went on to build a major steppingstone in the laboratory of history, those few places where freedom was tested and succeeded. Revel writes that "Athens, Rome, Renaissance Italy, eighteenth-century England and France—all were societies of this type, not as a result of some abstract 'process,' but because of human deeds."[41] They are referred to in this book as "stepping stones" because they blazed the trail for free people one after the other for almost 4000 years, starting with the Phoenicians and extending today to places all around the world. It is remarkable how from these small ancient beginnings the political and economic foundations of today's many democracies were established. Professor Hanson has described well their origins:

> "These farmers revolutionized the economic and cultural life of their fellow Greeks and left as their legacy the idea that small, family-centered production, on family property, was the most efficient and desirable economic system; that the farmers' creed could be successfully superimposed on the entire community... that like-minded people could band together in novel self-supporting communities to ensure their personal liberty and equality."[42]

That ancient free Greek culture persisted for over five centuries, illustrating the unique effectiveness of their democratic city-states, their inquisitive scientists, their dramatic theaters, and a strong patriotism that resisted the recurring invasions of the Persian Empire. Professor R.J. Hopper has reported that "the Greeks had the best of both worlds; they were themselves free of the autocratic and theocratic institutions of the Middle East, but they could draw on its accumulated observations."[43] Notably, they adopted and improved the Phoenician alphabet, and writing was "emancipated from the influence of a professional class of scribes, and suited to the common need for a form of writing which *everyone* might use…"[44]

Hippocrates, born 460 BC, was one of the first doctors to believe that disease wasn't a punishment from the gods.

In that way, and because they were free, the early Greeks could take innovative ideas from other communities, adapt them, and make use of them. Their scientists initiated the study of medicine. Those same ideas, in autocratic societies, often were left undeveloped because most individuals had neither the liberty nor inclination to develop them.

However, after 500 years, at its zenith of opulence and intellectual powers, the Greek cities weakened. Their demise was accelerated by a prolonged war with Sparta and a failed battle to control Sicily.

Demoralized by these defeats, the people fell under the influence of Plato's aristocratic clique that sought to restore autocratic authority over their unruly democratic populace. Those upper classes had been increasingly influenced by Sophist doctrines challenging the traditional democratic spirit of Athens, and along with a lingering resentment of the masses, "provided the oligarchs with a convenient justification for the violence they used to overthrow the democracy in 411 BC and again in 404 BC."[45] Democracy was restored but their cultural beliefs and unity had been broken, class divisions widened, and the cities of Greece declined in power and influence.

THE RISE AND FALL OF ROME

The vacuum left was soon filled by the Roman people. The original Romans got their start in a small rural area in central Italy and gradually spread into ever-larger territories, until they dominated the Italian peninsula. The early Romans established their Republic in 510 BC by overthrowing their king, Tarquin the Proud. Professors Acemoglu and Robinson write that then, "The republic cleverly designed political institutions with many inclusive elements."[46] What lucky people they were to have a clever republic!

Obviously, it would be more accurate to give credit to the founding people who actually designed and implemented those institutions. But most scholars appear resistant to the simple fact that people did it; a curious reluctance to be explored in coming chapters! In fairness to Daren Acemoglu, the text box shows a quote I recently found where he comes a little closer to crediting people for those beneficial institutions, although his words still avoid any direct attribution and say the institutions emerged as the outcome of a conflict between elites and "others."

WHO DESIGNS INSTITUTIONS?

Inclusive economic and political institutions do not emerge by themselves. They are often the outcome of significant conflict between elites resisting economic growth and political change and those wishing to limit the economic and political power of existing elites.

DAREN ACEMOGLU

Those early Romans that designed the helpful institutions subsequently enjoyed great success for over 400 years. However, during those 400 years the elites grew in power and eventually began sending the Plebeians to fight extended wars in foreign lands. During the soldiers' prolonged absence, the elites were soon tempted to confiscate their "abandoned" farms.[47] It was not long before the gradual increase in the elites' power had brought the citizens to a boiling point.

The people, loving their freedom, were not going to give in to the elites without a fight. In 133 BC they managed to elect Tiberius Gracchus as their tribune, a man "with an impeccable aristocratic pedigree," and one who agreed with them that land reform was needed to bolster the rights of the common Roman citizens. Tiberius proposed to have a commission determine if public land was being illegally occupied and to find a way to redistribute land holdings over 300 acres to landless Roman citizens.

Naturally, the Senate establishment wanted none of that, so they arranged to have Tiberius clubbed to death and his body thrown into the Tiber River. Former supporters of Tiberius who continued the fight were ruthlessly suppressed, and discord persisted, leading to the Social War (91–87 BC). It was a common theme: the common people may fight for their rights, but the elites never give up!

Forty years later, when Julius Caesar returned from the wars in Gaul, with his victorious army, the elites knew he was sympathetic to all former soldiers and their need for land. So, they told him to stop and not cross the bridge over the Rubicon. Caesar ignored that suggestion and moved in, but in 44 BC he was murdered, civil war broke out, and the Roman Republic was never restored. The Fall of Rome happened gradually after that period as the elites tightened their grip over the nation. Ordinary working people had built Rome, and the people in the elite ranks brought it down. It's always all about the people!

> "The ultimate resource is people—skilled, spirited, and hopeful people who will exert their wills and imaginations for their own benefit, and so, inevitably, for the benefit of all."
>
> ~ JULIAN SIMON

After a decade of civil wars, at Actium in 31 BC, Augustus Caesar won the crown and brought order for the next forty-five years, and Rome continued as a world power for another century. However, the partially inclusive institutions that had existed were continually undermined by the Senate elites. "The changes unleashed by Augustus, as with the Venetian Serrata, were at first political but would have significant economic consequences…. By the fifth century the Western Roman Empire…had declined economically and militarily and was on the brink of collapse."[48]

Before long the numerous Germanic tribes, led by such audacious leaders as Attila the Hun, enjoyed a centuries-long period of marching south to sack Rome.

This pattern of a successful society being eventually derailed by an elite was not just established in Greece and Rome. Professors Acemoglu and Robinson write: "The decline of Rome had causes very similar to those of the Maya city-states. Rome's increasingly extractive political and economic institutions generated its demise because they created disunity, infighting and civil war."[49] Those two authors describe institutions as either extractive or inclusive, meaning that the former help elites extract excessive wealth for themselves, and the latter allow ordinary people to be included in the production and the sharing of a community's wealth.

Acemoglu and Robinson explain that it was the extractive institutions that "generated" Rome's collapse. But that's only a partial truth. It was the elites—living, breathing, selfish leaders—who altered the once beneficial and inclusive institutions to benefit themselves. (Murdering Gracchus and Caesar and other dissidents helped, too!) It was purely such actions taken by the elites that caused the decline.

That may seem like a small distinction, but by accepting the fact that only people can make things happen, we make the interpretation of history not only more accurate but more useful. The move from inclusive to extractive institutions cannot just happen! Only people can make them change for better or worse. And it is certainly more informative to know that Rome's demise wasn't caused by a mysterious and unexplained change in institutions and laws, but by the selfish deeds of its elites who changed the rules!

Once institutions are made less inclusive, the role of the common people is reduced, their motivation declines, the nation loses the creative power of its people, the rich get richer, the people get poorer, and they either revolt or fall into an apathetic dependent state of mind. In short, institutions function for better or worse exactly as the people who designed them want them to act.

Most problems for democracies have come when the people's efforts to maintain or restore their rights failed; many of them then lost their confidence in the government and its leaders, and a debilitating apathy set in. The civic unrest, the protests by the people, and the eventual slide into dependency were the result of the elite's suppression of the people! Venice, Rome, and the Mayans all fell to similar parasitic practices of their elites.

VENICE—THE QUEEN CITY OF THE DARK AGES

Perhaps the purest example of a start-up nation, with a high degree of equality and an elaborate system of political representation for its people, was seen in the story of Venice. Like ancient Greece, freedom and equality was not enjoyed by all—women had fewer rights than men, and slaves had even fewer. But all the land-owning males met in open assembly to shape the workings of their community. It was only a partial victory for the common folks, but the seeds of full democratic states was sowed for future elaboration.

Venice had its beginning in the fifth century, when the Roman Empire was collapsing. The Roman citizens living along the northeast coast of Italy found themselves directly in the path of successive waves of barbarians from the north on their way to sack Rome. In order to escape those invaders, many families started the move to the remote swampy lagoons along the Adriatic Sea where they could find safety. Those tidelands were unoccupied, mosquito-infested, and inaccessible–the barbarians would pass them by, preferring the riches to be found in Rome itself. Christopher Hibbert has described these original settlers who paddled out into a new land with their earthy possessions bundled into tiny boats that could be rowed through the shallow channels where few could follow:

> "Unlike the inhabitants of terra firma…all classes lived on equal terms, occupying the same kind of dwellings, and eating the same food. Envy, the vice which rules the world, was unknown to them. As the years passed, they developed a kind of federation, each community electing representatives to a central authority…and in the first half of the eighth century they appointed a leader."[50]

For the next 900 years, the people of Venice elected a leader to oversee the government. This was truly a "start-up" nation, free of domineering elites, and its people used their freedom to build one of history's crown jewels.

John Ruskin described this initial arrangement as "an aristocratic society of famous stability, dependent on mutual trust between its classes, and intensely patriotic...the Britain of its day, mistress of a maritime empire built on trade and technology."[51] The Venetian Republic became the pride of Europe, dominating trade in the eastern Mediterranean Sea, and resisting all efforts of the Turks and Islamic forces to take over the Western stronghold of Italy.

The Venetian people, like the Phoenicians before them, were short on land and natural resources, so they concentrated their efforts in trading activities. The merchants created a large, prosperous middle class that kept close watch over their liberty, and this prevented any elite from forming a parasitic burden on their free market activities. From 697 AD to 1797 AD the city elected 120 doges, and for the first six of those centuries were quick to depose, exile, or murder any of those who tried to assume too much power.

Those citizens were not passive subjects. As Mancur Olson reminds us, "In Venice, after a doge who attempted to make himself an autocrat was beheaded for his offense, subsequent doges were followed in official processions by a sword-bearing symbolic executioner as a reminder of the punishment intended for any leader who attempted to assume dictatorial power.... The same city states also tended to have more elaborate courts, contracts, and property rights than most of the European kingdoms of that time. As is well known, those city states also created the most advanced economies in Europe, not to mention the culture of the Renaissance."[52]

Machiavelli, a shrewd advisor to the powerful Renaissance families that occasionally did assume great powers, warned such "Princes" to do as they might, but do not mess with the people's private property: "Do not arouse hatred in the people, something he can avoid 'if he does not touch the goods and the women of his citizens and subjects.'"[53]

WISE ADVICE TO A PRINCE

"When you disarm the people, you commence to offend them and show that you distrust them either through cowardice or lack of confidence, and both of these opinions generate hatred."

~ NICCOLO MACHIAVELLI

By heeding that advice, many less than democratic nations have worked fairly well for their citizens as long as the latter enjoyed an open and free economy and secure property rights. One might well ask, who needs a vote if you have a good job and a house, free economic rights, and the safety of your family and property? After all, the only need for a government is to provide such safety and opportunity. The vote only helps keep the elites from limiting those fundamental elements of personal happiness.

If elites were benign there would be no need for democracies and all that voting and campaigning. The fact is that the major reason we have elections is because elites are rarely good to their people! Consequently, voters must pay attention and choose well in order to keep their leaders from stealing too much or imposing too many restrictions on their liberty. Renaissance cities, which did swing between democratic and semi-authoritarian rule, may have owed their success to the continuing provision of some basic rights to their people. The elites were wise and therefore somewhat benign. They must have heard the adage that it is one thing to be a pig but quite another to be a total hog!

If there is one thing to be learned from the Venetian experience, it is that it is wise to have the elite, the doge himself, always exposed to serious censure should he exceed his authority. The Venetian system worked admirably for many centuries, but eventually it too fell victim to its elite.

SUMMARY

Those four free civilizations, all located in the Mediterranean region where Europe and Asia meet, had the advantage of close proximity to each other, allowing the constant cross-fertilization of their people's many discoveries. Their time of greatness spanned 3,000 years, roughly from 1500 BC to 1500 AD, the period when mankind gradually discovered that ordinary citizens could push the elites aside and do even better without them.

Centuries later, the American founders still had to look back to those winning examples to shape their own democratic republic. Those ancient people showed that it could be done, but it could have happened anywhere, and has subsequently happened in every corner of the world, as evidenced by the recent *Indices of Economic Freedom*.[54] The reason it didn't happen elsewhere is that almost all other people were tightly controlled by the despots ruling over great empires.

Freedom creates not only patriotic pride and a unity among its people, but it is able to draw on and benefit from the initiative and creativity of many. That is because free and open economies bring out the best from a wide swath of people and unleash a productivity and creativity far beyond what a totalitarian society can hope to muster.

Those unique societies suggest that any People who establish an open and free economy, provide for the Safety of their lives and property, and avoid Oppression, will gain Prosperity, Liberty, and maybe even Happiness. I have referred to this before as "The Radzewicz Rule." It's almost as simple as second-grade arithmetic:

People + Safety – Oppression = Prosperity

No abstract theories needed!

In the next chapter we will review the work of historians and economists who have struggled to explain the Rise and Fall of Nations. Hint: they have all come up short because the truth contradicts their claim that the elites created the progress of Rising nations.

CHAPTER 4-

Why Experts Have Failed to Explain the Rise and Fall of Nations

 *"A whole new class of intellectuals has arisen to supply a history geared to what people currently wish to believe, rather than to the record of the past."*

Thomas Sowell, Race and Culture

O**N THE BIG QUESTION, THE** reason for the rise and fall of nations, the experts have suggested many different possibilities but no clear answer. Professor Gregory Clark's excellent and informative book, *A Farewell to Alms*, surveys almost all the attempts to answer that question, but, at the end, avoids any conclusion: "The West has no model of economic development to offer the still-poor countries of the world. There is no simple economic medicine that will guarantee growth... Even direct gifts of aid have proved ineffective in stimulating growth."[55]

How can all these writers miss the point? Every one of the several Indices of Economic Freedom and Human Rights, for every year of the past few decades, make it clear that per capita income varies directly with the economic freedom and human rights enjoyed by the people. The correlation comes close to the certainty frequently available in the physical sciences!

Clark provides a wealth of data on the rapid increase in productivity in England from 1750–1850 but never mentions the individuals who, by tinkering with machinery, achieved those gains. That omission, not looking for the individuals who created the new age of machinery, has been a common weakness among the scholars studying the broad pattern of history. They present an immense amount of statistical data but there is no attempt to look behind the numbers to determine who made those technical advances.

If we look closely at those writers, we can see why they failed. Some wise person once said that those who don't participate directly in the real world, and thus know little about it, are the ones who write. Those people actually doing things in the real world don't have time to write about it. Consequently, those who write are both inexperienced and uninformed. Plus, many of the academics and economists want to take credit for all progress. And, perhaps, due to an intellectual arrogance, they cannot imagine that common people caused progress—if inexperience and conceit does not cloud their eyes, self-interest will.

SEARCHING IN VAIN FOR THEORETICAL ANSWERS

In an earlier chapter, we related how a couple historians suggest that strong "inclusive" institutions rather than geographic, cultural, or market-based factors are the primary reasons why nations succeed or fail. What they mean by "strong inclusive institutions" is that if the laws and financial institutions provide opportunity to a large portion of the people, the economy will do well. Conversely, when participation in such activities is "exclusive," that is, available to only a small segment of the citizenry, the nation will do poorly. Without specifically saying it, they are almost suggesting that it is the people at large who make things happen but only if they have the freedom to do so.

Such examples of an apparent reluctance to credit people for a nation's success was given in the preceding chapter concerning the founding of Rome: The authors attributed success to how "the republic cleverly designed political institutions with many inclusive elements."[56] But "republics" can't write—they have no hands or brains, they are not "clever," and they're illiterate! In fact, it was the people who established the institutions that allowed them to build a great free republic.

Even Ludwig Von Mises, a noted conservative economist by trade and a great intellectual by nature, made a similar mistake: For example, he wrote this concerning the Industrial Revolution:

> "The tremendous progress of technological methods of production and the resulting increase in wealth and welfare were feasible only through the pursuit of those liberal policies which were the practical application of the teachings of economists.... None of the great modern inventions would have been put to use if the mentality of the pre-capitalistic era had not been thoroughly demolished by the economists. What is commonly called the 'industrial revolution' was an offspring of the ideological revolution brought about by the doctrines of the economists."[57]

Thus, he offered a simple clear answer: the economists created the Industrial Revolution; they did it with their "doctrines" that provided the base for successful economies. The only flaw in that explanation is that innovative societies had existed long before the economists developed their doctrines! The printing press was one "of the great modern inventions" and it was quickly "put to use" in 300 European towns by 1500. And it was not an "invention" but represented a primitive machine created in China that had been subjected to many small modifications by hundreds of European mechanics so that the printing process gradually became increasingly efficient.

Such advances in technology had begun thousands of years earlier when cavemen and women first made use of levers, inclined planes, pulleys, and created the wheel. Economists had nothing to do with it. Clever individuals, empowered by a liberty of action, developed many innovations and that process had been going on long before there were any economists!

Karl Marx: He suggested the Holocaust

Unfortunately, other theorists have followed Von Mises in crediting economic theories for the success of nations. But they offer different theories! Von Mises had opened the proverbial can of worms. For example, Karl Marx suggested his own theory of what would work best—a form of socialism or communism that he claimed would provide equality to the people and avoid the greed and waste of capitalistic systems. By stoking that utopian dream, and denigrating the free market, Marx advanced ideas that helped elites gain authoritarian control. However, because those authoritarians did not like too many classes of people, his guidance resulted in the death of millions of Russian peasants.

HE SUGGESTED THE HOLOCAUST

"The classes and the races too weak to master the new conditions...must perish in the revolutionary Holocaust.

KARL MARX, 1856

Quite differently, Johan Norberg's recent book *Progress* makes it clear that the reason why poverty was endemic for most of human history was "the absence of freedom." Norberg is optimistic about the future and cites the great recent progress in the availability of food in most every nation. According to the UN's Food and Agricultural Organization, in 1947 about 50 percent of the world's population was chronically malnourished. By 1970 they estimated that 37 percent of the developing world population was undernourished, and today the figure is about 13 percent. "Despite what we hear on the news and from many authorities, the great story of our era is that we are witnessing the greatest improvement in global living standards ever to take place."[58]

The progress we see comes from a very real expansion of freedom around the world. There is a clear implication in Norberg's words that people produce such progress if they have the freedom to act in a creative manner. But even he does not make it clear that people do it. The need to zero in on people as the active agents for progress is that the nature of the freedom enjoyed, and the structure of the enabling institutions, can best be measured simply by whether 1) they provide direct help to the initiative and motivation of *all* their people, 2) they are only minimally restrictive to the peoples' enterprise, and 3) they prevent unfair trading advantages for any participants.

Those are the three obvious requirements for a "free enterprise" economy. Today's elites have done their best to subvert all three: They have tried to lessen the peoples' initiative, restrict those who want to participate, and insert laws that help themselves gain a preferential advantage. The result for many nations is "crony capitalism," a corrupted form of free markets. It's like a basketball game with crooked referees paid to favor one team over the other!

PAST ATTEMPTS TO EXPLAIN

Jeffrey Sachs, whose history textbooks are used in many public high schools, has at least discounted the importance of geography and environmental factors. Instead, he looked to social conditions and governmental policies: "...economic development requires a government oriented towards development...the government must create an environment conducive to investments by private businesses."[59]

What that actually means is that a government must stand back and allow its people to innovate by not imposing obstacles. And he attributes England's Industrial Revolution to their society being "relatively open, with more scope for individual initiative and social mobility...their institutions of political liberty...traditions of free speech and open debate...(and) increasingly powerful protectors of private property rights, which in turn underpinned individual initiative."[60] Sachs thus does look to the valuable supporting factors that both allowed and motivated people to apply their talent and build a strong economy.

However, like all the experts he doesn't directly credit people for advancing affluence and he doesn't make clear that every one of those "supporting factors" was created by people. Historians all avoid that fact by glossing over how those institutions of political liberty and the protection of private property had originated. And they also do not make clear that it was the elites who had imposed and enforced the restrictions on initiative, free speech, and private property rights.

Now some historians and economists do suggest the source of inclusive institutions, but they usually credit John Locke and other Enlightenment philosophers who wrote their generalized tomes on "freedom" in the last few centuries. However, the printing press and many other technical advances occurred during the early to late Medieval period, long before economists appeared. In short, ordinary working people not only built the machines that marked the Industrial Revolution, but they had to first overcome the oppressive elites and shape an environment that allowed them to do so! The common people did it all—against the constant opposition of the entrenched elites.

The weakness of historians and economists is that they love theoretical concepts and approach the question why some nations did better than others as an abstraction. They generalize about contributory factors and suggest that institutions helped create success; or perhaps it was good climate, navigable rivers, natural resources, available beasts of burden, maybe the culture, good luck, or even guns, germs, and steel? However, climate and guns can do nothing—they are inanimate.

Cultures didn't invent the steam engine, navigable rivers never engaged in trade, and Kenya and its rolling savannas never won a marathon. Empowering laws and institutions are created by people, and people invent, perfect, and manufacture guns and steel. If there is a common thread—and it is really so simple—it is that people, make it all happen!

We needn't even look at historical cases to know this because there is nothing else on earth that could create gardens, tools, or institutions except humans! Therefore, the question becomes: Why have some humans been able to succeed better than others? We know that it was rarely a matter of their geography because great successes have been seen in unfavorable settings, such as Venice, the Andes, Israel, and Japan, and relative failures have occurred in many benign settings all around the globe.

This question terrifies all politically correct academics who fear being called "racist" if they talk about the role of people. However, the explanation presented in these pages may involve people but is not racist. We know that people all around the globe are succeeding in every place where they have adopted the mechanics of free and open societies. Every ethnic group does appear equally adept at succeeding in the business world if they gain the freedom to do so!

Thus, people of all races are equal, and they are equally capable of creating prosperous economies. What's more, the elites of every race are all equally able to mess it all up. History reveals those two facts. When it comes to building nations, or crippling them, we can best see the total equality of mankind: people of every ethnicity are equally adept at both making or breaking their country!

THEORETICAL ANSWERS VERSUS ACTUAL CASES

Today's experts, it seems, find themselves on the horns of a dilemma—a situation in which they have to choose between two explanations that are equally unpleasant to themselves: Many of them used to assert that success was gained by the "superiority" of a few ethnic groups, (a racist argument), but that became untenable. And they cannot bring themselves to admit the real answer: that success could have been attained by any group of people who had the freedom to act purposefully as proposed in this book. That admission would concede that they, the experts, were not involved, that ordinary people created great communities and that such communities were formed long before economists and social scientists started writing about it. The only way they can preserve their leadership role is to maintain this ridiculous debate about whether such things as navigable rivers, guns, or beasts of burden were the agents that built our homes, boats, medicines, and spaceships! Incredibly, they have never been called out before on this massive charade and cover-up!

In brief, there were always two types of obstacles standing in every community's way: either a disadvantage from those many geographic factors the historians write about or people on the inside or outside who suppressed the freedom of the citizens to act. History shows that people have been far more able to compensate for poor climate and geography than to protect themselves from outside enemies and internal elites.

THE NEED FOR SAFETY OF PERSONS AND PROPERTY

Many of the writers attempting to explain why the Industrial Revolution "happened" in Europe get lost in the details and indicate that there are too many factors involved to permit a clear explanation. For example, one of the best, E. L. Jones, writes: "Pulling this complex of conditions apart does not find us an 'engine of growth.' The pattern, not a single magic change, was what 'brought down the bird.' A relatively steady environment and above all, the limits to arbitrariness set by a competitive political arena do seem to have been the prime conditions of growth and development. Europe escaped the categorical dangers of giant centralized empires as these were revealed in the Asian past. Beyond that, European development was the result of its own *indissoluble, historical layering*."[61] (Italics added.)

Bill Radzewicz: Creator of "The Radzewicz Rule." A 2nd generation immigrant, who loved America for its Safety and Freedom

Buried in that vague and hesitant conclusion, Jones is stating that there were two "prime conditions of growth," namely: a "steady environment" (safety) and "limits to arbitrariness" (less oppression).

That is what the Radzewicz Formula states in a simpler and more direct manner:

People (+ Safety – Oppression) = Economic freedom = Prosperity

Or

People (+ S – O) = Prosperity

Jones is correct in describing safety and less oppression as being "conditions of growth," not the cause of growth. But let's look deeper at what he's saying: "Safety" is clearly the safety of people, and "limits to arbitrariness" has to mean less regulation of the people. He isn't implying we need safety for plants or less regulation of animals. So, why do we need the safety of people and freedom for people? Because only people can make things happen. Without clearly saying so, Jones appears to give individual people the credit for the success of nations.

Another way of thinking of this is to visit once again the legendary Garden of Eden, with its bountiful environment and not a whit of oppression. But nothing significant could happen there until people arrived. That is why our equation starts with a "P" for people. All they need is to establish a bit of safety and freedom and they will do all sorts of great stuff!

Professor Jones' detailed and informative book, published in 1987, comes close to confirming that people make it all happen if they gain safety and a degree of economic freedom. More recent books, influenced by the growing demands of political correctness, have been more apt to give credit to the environment, institutions, exploitation of colonies, and even luck and guns, always carefully avoiding any reference to the role of people.

The weakness of such recent explanations is that the fear of political correctness, or a personal attack for being racist, has increasingly chained the minds of most academics. Jared Diamond explained that his major motivation in writing *Guns, Germs and Steel* was that "until we have some convincing, detailed agreed-upon explanation for the broad pattern of history, most people will continue to suspect that the racist biological explanation is correct after all."[62]

Diamond's book, however, still did not come up with a "convincing, detailed agreed-upon explanation." Many readers, however, may have assumed from the title that the Western European nations' use of guns, germs, and steel cutlasses to colonize the world's people caused their rise to world supremacy. However, the reality is that the West's possession of such overpowering technologies as guns, steel, and fleets of world-circling ships was very clear proof of their pre-existing technical supremacy.

It is certainly true that we need an agreed-upon explanation for a nation's success, but the explanation must be correct, because only if it is correct will it provide the means to help those nations that have fallen behind. It is critical to recognize that the source of a nation's success is its people and to act purposefully they need some degree of freedom and opportunity. And it's equally important to recognize that any people can do it—it's already happening in the African and Asian nations mentioned in this book. The cruel crime being committed is the refusal of economists and historians to agree on that obvious cause of success.

It is the intention of this book to explain:

1) that "the broad pattern of history" has been determined by people (not guns, rivers, arable land, or the consumption of tea),

2) that significant advances could have been achieved by any of the people on earth,

3) that most people were denied the chance to create progress by the parasitic burden of their elites, and,

4) that the people of poorer nations can only be helped by finding leaders who will allow their people the freedom, safety, and institutional support that will let them build a strong economy.

SUMMARY

The fate of mankind was determined by the fact that we were blessed with free will, brains to innovate, common sense to make improvements, hands to craft tools, and the good sense to form communities with laws and institutions that magnified our efforts. And we did just that. Without us, all the natural resources on earth would have remained undeveloped and the fertile soil untilled.

We don't know if a God was involved, kind or capricious, but because we were able to act, and able to think, we were free. Exulting in that freedom, mankind has rejoiced, progressed, and at times slid backward. But without that free ability to make choices, dream big dreams, we would have been no different than the colonized bees and ants, living in a constant state of rigid genetic impulses, destined to merely collect food and trace a predetermined life. No wonder many people praise God, for somehow our path has been able to soar to unimaginable achievements and wonder, even if marked by the follies and avarice of the many Cains among us.

Let no one take away our achievements for they have been remarkable, unique on this planet, and they offer a future of equal splendor. Let's have no more of that stuff like "you didn't build that," nor that nonsense about how the climate, the geography, or the government did it. We did it—ordinary, work-a-day men and women did it all—and it's up to us to continue the onward march for our children and their children's sake.

SUMMARY OF PART I

Mankind's History of Oppression and Wars

About one-hundred and fifty years ago, Abraham Lincoln gave the world's people one of the most famous messages in history. It was a speech that lasted only a couple minutes and he only needed 269 well-chosen words to make his point: Freedom is a blessing that only comes from a government FOR the people, and we all must struggle to hold onto our liberty lest it "perish from this earth."

In the preceding pages the reader has seen how such free nations, where most of the citizens avoided a life of servitude under despotic elites, were created when people started a new community free of the tyrannical rules and customs inevitably imposed by ruling classes. That successful model was clearly demonstrated by how those pioneers in liberty built some of the most illustrious societies in history.

However, even in America, the quintessential land of the free, the battle for freedom never ends. In his famed speech at Gettysburg, Lincoln echoed history's call for human rights, first heard 2500 years ago in ancient Judea and Athens. However, the elites never sleep; they have now raised their sights on a greater prize–to gain control over all Americans, regardless of race or merit, and thereby extinguish the flame of freedom for all those they consider "deplorable."

Never forget that elites never liked Lincoln. They work full time to ensure that governments of the people, by the people, and for the people will quickly and finally "perish from this earth."

THE PARASITIC ROLE OF ELITES

PART II

The Progression of Freedom & Knowledge
(1000 AD—1750 AD)

CHAPTER 5-

How Freedom Spread: Iceland, Holland, Norway, Switzerland, et. al.

"A number of human convictions have persisted ever since civilization began, little changed by the passage of time; these seem to be permanent truths, which any civilized nation must reckon with or decay."

~ Russell Kirk

FORTUNATELY, THE "STEPPINGSTONES TO FREEDOM" did not end with the demise of those earliest democracies described in chapter three. Many communities in Europe carried on their legacy of free governance. Even after Rome fell, during the so-called "Dark Ages," from 500–1000 AD, places like Venice thrived as free republics. In other parts of the world, dominating elites and oppressive belief systems continued to hold their people in servitude. That differing degree of liberty was to determine the future success of Western countries over all others for the next 1000 years.

A little recognized example was displayed for all Europeans to see in the late ninth century when Viking farmers settled Iceland. Their arrival coincided with a period of global warming and they found a verdant but uninhabited land with rich fields to cultivate. They established homes and farms and soon gathered together in 874AD to organize one of the first representative parliaments in European history.[63] They were early democrats, but there soon were others; similar parliaments had been established by 1300AD in small communities on the islands and coastal cities of Scotland, Germany, Estonia, and Lithuania. These Medieval trading cities were allied by mutual business activities in the Hanseatic League, which kept the benefits of freedom obvious to everyone throughout the area.

The people of these locales had an advantage over most other people of the world. They not only were not subjected to the severe oppression of Asiatic empires, but they were connected by active trade routes, and were familiar with the principles shaping free communities. The Renaissance cities of Italy that blossomed from 1000 to 1600 AD also enjoyed the relative freedom seen in Venice and were the homes of the world's first universities, where Franciscan and Dominican monks began the gradual scholarly separation of science from the spiritual world.

These new steppingstones spread throughout Europe and allowed their people to create a rapid acceleration in art, technology, music, and government. A clear pattern of progress had been thus established in Europe by 1400AD, and those advances nourished a gradual development culminating in "The Industrial Revolution."

Vilhelm Moberg has written about three other isolated and inhospitable lands where the people organized institutions that nourished their freedom: Sweden, Norway, and Switzerland. The Swiss League was formed in 1291 and "behind the magnificent ramparts of their mountains its people defended themselves successfully and preserved their freedom…. In Norway's mountains and deep valleys, the Norwegian peasants, too, had dwellings inaccessible to outside interference. Mounted men-at-arms found no roads to advance by. Nor had the country any indigenous nobility; and the Danish nobles were few in number, and thereto extremely remote from their own capital in Copenhagen. To keep the Norwegians under effective surveillance was beyond the power of the Danish overlords."[64]

The people of Holland followed those early pioneers of freedom by occupying tidal lowlands undesired by the major surrounding powers. They did eventually have to fight the claims of the king of Spain, but after they won that battle, they fashioned a free and prosperous nation for themselves. The Hague's local assembly of merchants and traders began the Dutch revolution in 1581 when they issued the "Oath of Abjuration" that set forth what had become a fundamental principle of government: Because King Philip of Spain had violated the obligation of a ruler to be fair to his subjects, they had the right "to withdraw their allegiance and depose an oppressive and tyrannical sovereign."[65] Those Dutch Burghers won the war and started up one of the most successful nations in history.

THE OATH OF ABJURATION

"It is apparent to all that a prince is constituted by God to be ruler of a people, to defend them from oppression and violence as the shepherd his sheep, and whereas God did not create the people slaves to their prince...when he does not behave thus, but on the contrary, oppresses them...then he is no longer a prince, but a tyrant, and the subjects are to consider him in no other view..."

RATIFIED: JULY 26, 1581

THE HAGUE, HOLLAND

It is noteworthy that the ancient Judeo-Greek legacy of democratic institutions had been established thousands of years earlier: A nation's people could indeed remove a tyrant who did not respect their rights. However, the fact that such free communities arose so very rarely indicates how difficult it was to escape the domination of elites. But the people in those free "start-up" nations had found ways to gain liberty; they designed enabling institutions and laws and, they did it long before the American settlers first arrived in the New World. They provided both the inspiration and the legal and financial knowledge that those Americans used when fashioning their own free country. And that was all done before the earliest Enlightenment philosophers were born.

WHY THE STRUGGLE FOR FREEDOM NEVER ENDS

In sixteenth-century Europe, Martin Luther struck a fatal blow to any claim for the "Divine-Right of Kings." After that, aristocracies got weaker, and the common people gained added liberty. But freedom never came easily; the American colonists would have to repeat the Dutch struggle 200 years later when they fought to escape the authority of their king.

Barbara Tuchman commented on such persistence to gain freedom from unjust elites, which form a long historical sequence, whether in the fourth century BC in Rome, the fourth century AD Venice, sixteenth century Holland, or eighteenth century America: "Men's instinct for liberty, and belief in the people's right to depose a ruler who has governed unjustly, travels in deep common channels."[66] Those "deep channels" extend back hundreds, thousands of years, and display the enduring struggle for individual rights that has always pitted the ordinary people against those despots who would control them.

Those pioneers of liberty, the people who created all those stepping-stones to the future, had continually demonstrated by their deeds all the principles supporting freedom, human rights, and open economies. It was much later, only beginning in the late seventeenth century, that the Enlightenment "scholars" such as Locke, Rousseau, and Montesquieu wrote their complex treatises about the desirability of freedom. But those writers were merely playing catch-up with the common people, and even with hundreds, thousands, of pages, they set forth little more than the Dutch Burghers had made clear in their short and sweet *Oath of Abjuration* a couple centuries earlier.

Today's soft science "scholars" still revere the big thinkers and devote their lives trying to explain to their students what Locke meant in his supposedly monumental books. Like Rodney Dangerfield, the common people who had already been-there-done-that get little respect!

It is only by comparing the actual dates, when common people accomplished things, and when intellectuals wrote about them, that the readers of history will learn the true doers that shaped today's democratic states. Historian Pieter Geyl described the Oath of Abjuration as a "rather splendid, *albeit late*, expression of the sturdy medieval tradition of liberty,"[67] (Italics added) Thus the Dutch merchants, even in 1581, with their bold Declaration of Independence, were "late" in following in the footsteps of many earlier pioneers in liberty.

It is interesting that what Pieter Geyl was calling "late" was the demand for liberty, an idea clearly articulated almost 2000 years earlier, when Pericles described the immense advantage of democratic communities in his *Funeral Oration* delivered in 431 BC to the citizens of Athens.

It is almost unbelievable that we still have to fight the many opponents of freedom who propose regimes that would just be slight variations of despotism. That continuing debate is due primarily to the determination of elites to close any open and just economy so they can sit at the controls of a rigged system.

A RECENT START-UP: MODERN ISRAEL

It is a fact of history that many of the "steppingstones" to liberty, those communities that established a successful string of relatively free societies, had one thing in common: They were started by voluntary settlers who established a new home for themselves, making a fresh start, free of an oppressive establishment. A recent example has been described by authors Senor and Singer who titled their book *Start-Up Nation: The Story of Israel's Economic Miracle*.[68]

The Jews who flocked to settle their new homeland after WWII were an especially able and motivated group. They represented a modern equivalent of the first Venetians who ventured into the lagoons of the Adriatic coast in Italy and the Puritan/Calvinists/Quakers who ventured across the ocean to hack out homesteads from the rocky New England hills. They all wanted a new homeland, a free community, and, most of all, to escape the oppressive governments and limited economic hopes of their birthplaces.

The Israelis built a successful nation in record time by means of a mass movement of settlers into the newly formed nation of Israel. When the Cold War ended in the late 1980s, some 40 years after Israel was founded, Russian authorities could no longer stop the flood of people wanting to escape from the failed communist country. In the next ten years, about 800,000 Jews moved from Russia to Israel, increasing the country's population by about 20 percent.[69]

This mass exodus was a major blow to Russia and a boon to Israel. Although Jews had made up only two percent of Russia's population, they had represented about 25 percent of its doctors, engineers, and other professional classes. Those were "good" immigrants for Israel—competent, educated, and culturally like the people they joined. Of course, it is doubtful that Israel would have allowed hundreds of thousands of illiterates or culturally divisive people to enter their homeland!

Note that the Israeli example, one of many free and democratic nations, tells us that some free people succeed more than others. Senor and Singer ask: Why has Israel's extraordinarily innovative and successful entrepreneurship attracted the major technology companies from around the world to join the innovative activities in this small start-up nation? Why has such progress happened there and not somewhere else?

One partial answer is that adversity breeds unity and motivates people. Similar small countries such as Singapore, Taiwan, and South Korea can also boast growth records that are as impressive as Israel's. They share the same type of disciplined and capable workers, functioning in an open economy, but none of them have produced an entrepreneurial culture or an array of start-up companies to match what is seen in Israel.[70] The new Israel has been a virtual hotbed of innovative scientific advances, and in the next section we look for the reason.

HOW SOCIETIES BENEFIT FROM OPEN DEBATE

There are many nations with talented people, more engineers, and larger science schools than Israel. All around the world people are investigating current areas of innovation, but the major American companies do not set up mission-critical work in those countries. What they do in Israel is unlike anything they do anywhere else in the world. Authors Senor and Singer explain this mystery by pointing to the nature of Israel's cultural habits: What apparently separates Israeli people from most others in the world is their "chutzpah."

The word is borrowed from the ancient Yiddish language—it means gall, brazen nerve, presumption, plus arrogance—a combination of qualities that is never combined and communicated so effectively in any other language.[71] In Israel it describes how sergeants question their generals, students challenge their professors, employees speak with their bosses. To Israelis this isn't chutzpah; it's merely the normal way of working together. It is the exact opposite of "political correctness" which limits open and creative debate. Their frank and questioning mindset make the people of Israel different from others. That is why the leading tech companies in America—Google, Intel, Cisco, Microsoft—all go to Israel for their inspiration, new ideas, and to solve their worst technical problems.

Most other countries, even the democracies, are burdened by cultures that impose constraints on their people's behavior and attitudes. Those cultures discourage such questioning of authority and social informality. That censorship has been the ongoing work of their elites who have managed to stifle the hopes, dreams, and imagination of their people. Elites want to close minds and new ideas. It's called mental oppression.

KEEPING GOVERNMENT IN ITS PLACE

"The State is made for man, not man for the State."

~~ALBERT EINSTEIN

Note that *oppression* can be both physical and mental! That is why America's elites are trying to enforce politically correct chains on our voices: to silence opposition, to justify illegal immigration, to promote globalist organizations, to denigrate white males as racist, to convince the youth that America's historical record is evil and impose a silence on our past successes—all designed to enable their crusade to transform America, with them at the top, controlling everything the people do and even what they think. It is a type of thought control, the form of mental oppression that held back progress in the mighty Asian and Muslim nations for a thousand years. It is similar to the "Double Think" that George Orwell warned us about in his book *1984*.

The people of countries suffering under the burden of PC are *potentially* as capable and innovative as the people of all other nations. But that potentiality is chained, wasted, by the cultural code imposed by their elites. The result is that those unfortunate people are not able to accomplish the results of the people in Israel, who have made the desert bloom, the internet buzz, and their science and economy thrive. The Israeli people have enhanced their innate capabilities by a culture magnified by its chutzpah!

THE KEY ATTRIBUTES OF SUCCESSFUL NATIONS

There are five common features to be seen in the start-up success stories:

FIRST, they represent most of the nations in history where a large portion of the people attained a relatively high level of liberty.

SECOND, those people remained, at least for a time, unfettered by a large burdensome government or an oppressive clerisy that would slow them down.

THIRD, they were united and patriotic; highly motivated to form a strong military force to protect their freedom from aggressive neighbors.

FIFTH, the citizens formed legal systems and financial institutions that enhanced their ability to participate in an open economy, protected their private property, and penalized corrupt practices.

AND, finally, the people remained vigilant to keep oppressive elites from spoiling everything for as long as possible. Otherwise, the elites would have added restriction on the people and added loopholes in the laws to benefit themselves.

To remain successful, all the people of a nation need to do is to limit harmful regulations, work for unity and cooperative behavior, punish corruption, and reward those who truly contribute to the well-being of the people. No theories involved—just common honest good sense!

Sadly, in America today, the rules and regulations multiply like rabbits, the elites stir-up constant division and enmity, corruption at the highest levels runs rampant, and the major rewards too often go to the undeserving.

LESSONS FROM SWEDEN AND ENGLAND

Not all the people of Revel's "stepping-stones" were start-up nations. England had been a long-established nation when it led the Northern European nations' extraordinary advance into the miracles of the Industrial Revolution. That pathway was the more difficult because, as compared to a start-up, the people were oppressed from the start by landed gentry, intellectuals, and a king and his lords and ladies.

However, the English people had been shaped by ancestral freedom-loving Vikings, Celts, Anglo-Saxons, and the enabling laws of Roman invaders. They were familiar with the freedom enjoyed by the Swiss, Dutch, Norwegians, and the people living in the Italian Renaissance cities. They benefited from the Christian universities established by Catholic monks even before the Norman invasion. Their centers of learning at these universities were repositories of the best of European culture back to the ancient Greeks and Romans.

That heritage empowered the people to exert consistent pressure on their lords for rights to private property, jury trials, and a representative government. Their 500-year struggle for rights was reinforced in the sixteenth and seventeenth centuries by the fervor of active Protestant sects which believed their first loyalty was to God, not the king or his lordships.

Thus, the development of free countries has not been limited to just true start-up nations, where settlers arrived in virgin lands and created wholly new communities. History has witnessed many variations on every theme involving human activity, so broad generalizations are rarely useful. The development of freedom in England has been accomplished internally, by the efforts of many of its own residents, over a 900-year period, without massive revolutionary conflict.

Freedom in England was achieved in small increments, extracted ever-so-slowly by the common people from their well-ensconced elites. And, it may have been more the economic freedom that they gained, rather than political freedom, that gave them the unique advantage of being the center of the Industrial Revolution.

Sweden's history is much like England's, transforming itself first from an autocratic kingdom 400 years ago to a constitutional democracy. The value of free markets had become well-known throughout Europe during the seventeenth and eighteenth centuries. Indeed, Anders Chydenius, a Swedish pastor and teacher, anticipated Adam Smith's work in 1765 by publishing an essay explaining the benefits of an open marketplace. Sweden's free market-economy and its businesses prospered greatly during the Industrial Revolution and especially during the century leading up to 1950. But, in the 1970s, when the socialist party gained control, its economy suffered. After twenty years of subsequent economic decline, Sweden regained an open economy that has resulted in renewed growth. Johan Norberg describes this roller coastal ride:

> "Sweden, already one of the world's richest countries, went into decline during this (socialist) period and started lagging behind European and other global competitors. Not a single new job was created in the private sector. From being the 4th richest country in the world, it fell to 14th. Only one large private company was founded between 1970 and 2000. Real wages fell between 1975 and 1995 but then increased by almost 70% once the socialist policy experiment collapsed."[72]

Norberg points out that less developed nations can emulate Swedish economic success by adopting the open market and free trade policies that made Sweden rich. Fortunately, those enabling features are well known and have already been adopted wherever the elites have been kept from preventing it.

HOW CAPITALISM HAS EMBRACED WELFARE PROGRAMS

Norberg described the reforms that were needed to undo the harmful socialist policies: "Since 1990, Sweden has regained a successful economy by repealing the harmful socialist policies that had been put in place. The institutional modifications included deregulation, reduced welfare benefits, a national school voucher system, partially privatized pensions, reduced taxes overall, and the abolition of property tax and inheritance tax."[73]

Welfare was not eliminated because every capitalist country for centuries has provided a safety net for the needy. Thus, socialism cannot claim credit for its support of welfare because all economic systems are in agreement on the need for a safety net. It is governmental control of the business world that marks "socialism" and it is that extreme interference in the economy that makes socialist nations fail. It is welfare and disability assistance given out indiscriminately without adequate control that can be criticized as an unsustainable burden for any nation. As Norberg points out, Sweden has had to reduce such aid to remain solvent. Like everything, a sound welfare program should be run efficiently and fairly.

It is the nationalization of industry that distinguishes socialism, an extreme form of government seizure that was abandoned in both England and Sweden. A slightly less onerous form is excessive regulation of business which adds the bureaucratic inefficiency and poor decision-making of government officials to burden the otherwise more efficient management of private enterprises. Governments are destructive when they dictate management policies, but they are essential to maintain rules that keep the marketplace open to all on an equal footing.

There is nothing complex about all the "isms" of economics: Socialism, fascism, communism, and crony capitalism are all merely variations of an overly regulated economy. Their only difference from true capitalism is that the latter requires only sufficient regulation to ensure equal and fair access to all participants. This is not a matter of theory or abstract reasoning. It is self-evident that, first, free people, working in a fair environment, can most successfully apply their energy and talent to overcome all problems that arise, and second, there must be honest referees to make sure no one creates unfair advantages for a favored few.

Sweden's historic swings between an autocracy, a free economy, then a try at a socialist government, and the resulting need to scrap socialism, illustrates that a free economy is best for its people. The Swedes also showed that an alert voting public can remedy mistakes and lead the nation in a better direction. The ballot box allowed the Swedes to start over a couple times.

STARTING OVER IN DEVELOPED LANDS

A second type of start-over nations involves the introduction of new people into an established and relatively advanced community. The British contributed an enormous cultural and institutional blessing when they invaded the Chinese mainland and occupied the island of Hong Kong on January 25, 1841. China lost the war and had to cede Hong Kong to Britain, which became a Crown Colony under the Treaty of Nanking and gave England full control for 150 years until 1997 when Hong Kong was returned to Chinese control.

Under British rule that small enclave escaped the totalitarian dictates of mainland China, and its residents quickly embraced capitalism and its related legal principles originally developed by the people of the Western nations. That opportunity allowed its citizens to create one of the most vibrant and prosperous cities in the world, a major center of trade and international finance. Hong Kong has consistently ranked as No. 1 in the Heritage Society's annual Indices of Economic Freedom. Unfortunately, with the treaty expired, the ruling elites in Peking are currently trying to assert their dominance more than 170 years after the British colonial administration had set the people of Hong Kong on the road to freedom. Totalitarian elites seem to never give up their desire to dominate free people.

Although the British exerted considerable influence, the population remained primarily of Chinese ethnicity. Their enthusiastic adoption of Western capitalism, and the removal of the Chinese government's authority, distinguishes Hong Kong's transformation as a classic "start-over nation." Hong Kong's example also suggests that all members of Homo sapiens can prosper if given economic freedom, as long as they adopt or adapt some of the the cultural and institutional trappings developed over many centuries by the people of Western nations.

England, as a colonial power, attempted to bring those enabling institutions of government to other members of their colonial empire.

In India, the English colonial administration ruled for over a hundred years and many beneficial English institutions, including democratic elections, were adopted and maintained to this day. That contribution, which partly offset the hardships of existing as a colonial subordinate, is why D'nesh DeSouza once proclaimed, "Two cheers for colonialism." The example of Hong Kong's success and England's positive influence in India, New Zealand, and Australia was not lost on the Asian "tigers" that, after WWII, introduced free markets and democratic traditions into the Pacific "rim nations" of Japan, South Korea, Taiwan, and Singapore.

TWO CHEERS FOR COLONIALISM

"Recently, the Indian prime minister, Manmohan Singh, gave a speech at Oxford in which he gave two cheers for colonialism. He said India is growing fast and is on its way to becoming a superpower. How? Because the Indians speak English, they have technology, they have universities, they have property rights, they have democracy. And why do they have these things? They got them from the British."

D'NESH DESOUZA, MAY 10, 2010
NATIONAL REVIEW INTERVIEW
KATHRYN LOPEZ

However, most colonial powers had little interest in helping their foreign subjects, and their rule ended with little gain for those people.

In most cases the "freedom" from colonial masters only resulted in the rise of local elites who treated them little better, and sometimes worse, than the colonial powers had.

Most conquerors and invaders of history stole their victims' wealth and enslaved their people. That pillaging nature marked the Persian and Roman legions, the Spanish Conquistadors, German invaders of the two world wars, and the Japanese in mid-twentieth century China. To their credit, most of England's conquered colonies were treated considerably better, and in some cases like Hong Kong, India, and Singapore, their arrival contributed to progress for their people.

Similarly, in recent times, Western occupation forces in defeated nations brought beneficial results—the American army remained in Germany and Japan after WWII and forced democratic systems down their throats. Aside from Germany's failed attempt at democracy for ten years between the two world wars, neither country's people had ever experienced freedom since time began. Under American direction, the large government cartels in both nations were broken up, the elites partially disbanded, and both countries were transformed into prosperous and free democratic nations. After the Korean War, American influence did the same in South Korea.

Those success stories indicate that all people can succeed if they have the freedom to adopt the complementary systems that allow an open, vibrant, and free economy. Thus, there have been many nations that do not qualify as "start-up nations" but have managed to reinvent themselves. Taiwan, Chile, Singapore, Japan, and South Korea have done it well. They clearly owe much of their economic success to the replacement of long-standing oppression with the enabling free market and related institutions of the West. Those examples show the people of such despotic autocracies as North Korea, China, Russia, and Iran that they can also find a way to follow in that pathway to freedom. The West's leaders would be better employed by encouraging those oppressed people to stand up for their rights, rather than meeting with their autocratic rulers to sign meaningless climate accords and disarmament treaties.

ARE EDUCATED AND CULTURED PEOPLE NECESSARY?

The great innate potential of all humans makes it important to avoid overestimating the importance of a highly educated and culturally rich population. Granted, Israel possesses a high level of human capital, and that may explain the rapidity and extent of their success as a nation. But we also know of many nations that may have a considerably smaller proportion of engineers and scientists but have also succeeded way above the average.

Ruchir Sharma refers to such "start-overs" as *Breakout Nations.* He cites Uganda and Mozambique, often described in the 1980s, respectively, as the most sadistic and poorest nations on earth. "Yet, following decisive rebel victories in 1986 and 1994, both countries have achieved impressively strong growth. Mozambique was especially successful under the inspired leadership of Joaquim Chissano, who dumped socialism and voluntarily stepped down after his second term in office in 2014. Although those reforms pushed by Chissano have subsequently seen reversals, the economy is improving and drove growth to more than 7 percent in the last decade..."[74]

Thus, it can be done—a poor, oppressed people can turn their country around, quickly, by getting the right leadership and adopting the mechanics that make free enterprise sizzle. Recent examples abound as a growing number of nations in Africa demonstrate. Mauritius, Botswana, Rwanda, Cote d'Ivoire, Swaziland, and Uganda have been ranked 21, 34, 51, 75, 88, and 91 for attaining a classification as "mostly free or moderately free" out of more than 180 nations measured in the 2017 Index published by the Heritage Society.

Those five nations represent an extraordinary victory for all the common and oppressed people of the world: Even groups of people assumed to be handicapped culturally, enjoying minimal infrastructural advantages, with few bastions of educational excellence, have magically moved into the top half and are competing at an equal level with such countries as Japan 40, Hungary 56, France 72, Italy 79, Russia 114, and Greece 127. The magic ingredient: People, any people, if simply given the chance to apply their genius!

2017 INDEX OF ECONOMIC FREEDOM

THE HERITAGE FOUNDATION

# of nations	category	percent
5	Free	2.8%
29	Mostly Free	16.1%
59	Moderately Free	32.7%
64	Mostly Unfree	35.6%
23	Repressed	12.8%
180	Total	100.0%

Sharma also points to two Muslim nations that are coming on strong after adopting free market systems. "There are currently fifteen economies worth more than $1 trillion dollars a year, and the next two nations in line to join that elite group… are Muslim democracies with increasingly market-oriented economies: Indonesia and Turkey."[75] Their success could provide inspiration to other Muslim countries that continue to struggle under theocratic oppression.

SUMMARY

What we see in these exceedingly varied societies is that any community is able to gain freedom and then enjoy a greater prosperity for its people. All they need is to muzzle oppressive elites and abandon stifling cultural constraints. It is worth noting that all those "break-out" nations based their new economies on an open competitive capitalist format; not a single one of those success stories adopted a socialist economy.

Given the freedom to act, all people on earth can adopt the well-known enabling institutions that help advance their happiness and well-being. And, to repeat, the magic of that combination—freedom and a few supporting institutions and laws—has been demonstrated repeatedly for thousands of years. The basic rules for national success are not what The Great Gallagher would call "A totally new concept!" They are readily available to copy by any people that can push their oppressive elite aside.

CHAPTER 6-

How Freedom Led to a Steady Advance of Useful Knowledge

I have seen far because I have stood on the shoulders of giants.

~~ Isaac Newton

T HE MOST STRIKING THING SEEN in any review of the world's people and their communities is how varied their progress has been. We have discussed in earlier chapters how the Agricultural Revolution caused people in farming communities to keep records, a formality that hunter-gatherers never needed. The result was that those who settled down to farming were soon motivated by their circumstances to develop essential accounting and mathematical skills. Quite differently, hunter-gatherers continued relatively unchanged in Stone Age cultures to current times.

For several millennia, with science and technology in its infancy, the advance of the new agricultural societies was modest. However, by 2500 BC, the largest societies in China, India, and the Middle East were engaged in the beginnings of writing, mathematics, astronomy, and simple engineering. For the next 3,500 years, advances in science and technology continued slowly, with the most conspicuous improvements occurring in China, Greece, and the Roman empire. Other large nations also succeeded, but only by the sheer force of numbers and a strict control over their enslaved people. The extractive style of those despots explains how the Egyptians got the pyramids built and why only Emperors lived in splendid palaces surrounded by obedient servants and slaves.

Similarly, most Asian elites lived in luxury with servants handling the details, and like the Middle East potentates created magnificent palaces serviced by slaves and harems seized from conquered nations. Some scholars have praised the high level of sophistication seen in such despotic realms, but by today's standards, where the rights of the individual are more valued than the lifestyle of the rich and famous, those were not success stories. But, that extreme economic stratification of rulers and suppressed subjects had marked almost all communities on earth until the Phoenicians, Greeks, and Romans demonstrated a better way.

The reason that the Greeks of 800–300 BC stood out so clearly in those ancient times is that they lived in a comfortable style shared by most of their people and pioneered one of the first major breakthroughs in democratic government. Those ancient Greek people, free individuals, allowed to explore new possibilities, created a civilization still admired for its revolutionary sculpture, art, drama, architecture, and free assemblies. Nothing like it was allowed to happen anywhere else. Autocratic leaders had no desire to allow their people to do more than provide the ruling class with all the luxuries needed for their palatial lifestyle.

SCIENCE BECOMES SIGNIFICANT - 1100–1600 AD

Around 1100–1200 AD, everything changed, accelerated; there was a major turning point in the destiny of nations. The Judeo-Greek

heritage reappeared in Europe with universities and a growing awareness of human rights and open economies. Those empowering principles gradually freed the people so they could advance the technologies
and economies of their nations.

There were a number of political, economic, and social factors that made the European environment less oppressive than other
regions of the world and thereby allowed its people to engage in imaginative and creative enterprises. The fractured political scene, with
many small countries, created a greater degree of freedom and competition than was enjoyed by the people in colossal Asian Empires.
The monastic orders, with their universities and imaginative scholars,
encouraged new ways of thinking. Then, in the sixteenth century, the
Protestant Reformation splintered the power of religious authority and
allowed further advances in science and governance.

However, the many reasons for those opportunities "happening"
in Europe, and rarely anywhere else, is not critical for our purposes.
The essential point is that a slightly larger degree of freedom allowed
the European people to think freely, create, and make use of innovations. It was the absence of freedom in other parts of the world that
held back their people. Thus, it appears clear that while only people
can create progress, they require sufficient liberty to do so.

While a few universities did appear under Islamic rule, they
were devoted to religious scholarship, commentating on the Koran and
their faith. But in Europe, their peoples' ultimate success began with a
growing belief that they must separate the secular and religious worlds
so they could pursue the study of the physical sciences. Benedictine,
Dominican, and Franciscan monks opened over a dozen universities
in many of the largest European cities and set the foundations for eventual technical supremacy. The fact that this revolution in scholarship

and scientific experimentation was led by Catholic monks provides us with an insight into the importance of the Christian faith in the Rise of the West.

In the thirteenth century, Albertus Magnus, (Albert the Great), a Dominican friar, was studying the physical sciences and advancing the idea of natural law. "Even more so than his most famous student, St. Thomas of Aquinas, Albert's interests ranged from natural science all the way to theology. He made contributions to logic, psychology, metaphysics, meteorology, mineralogy, and zoology."[76] The University of Oxford was established in 1096, about a decade before Albert was born. a vivid illustration of how long ago the European advance in the "hard" sciences had its beginnings.

Albert the Great, b.1280 AD, was canonized by the Christian Church, which thereby endorsed his openness to truth, science, and reason, wherever it may be found.

Earlier in this book, the development of the wheel, more than 5000 years ago (possibly by a Fred Flintstone look-alike) was referred to as the beginning of the Industrial Revolution. Certainly, the geared windmills and catapults developed over 1500 years ago must be considered part of a continuing Industrial Revolution. Then, physical scientists active in European universities beginning 1000 years ago accelerated advances in the "hard" sciences. And after the Protestant Revolution in the 16th century, mechanical inventions created an explosive improvement in technological efficiency that has continued to this day. The point is that it is folly to try and name a date, or even a century, when the Industrial Revolution began. It was a long and gradual process, advanced by common people seeking to increase their power of action beyond pure manual labor. Philosophers, Enlightenment thinkers, and soft-science academics had little to do with it.

Meanwhile, in sharp contrast, the Chinese and Muslim world remained frozen in a self-imposed time warp. That stasis was not the fault of their people, who did create some revolutionary products such as the printing press, paper, and gunpowder. However, the emperors and sultans suppressed their use, and it was the Europeans who enthusiastically adopted them. In Germany, Johannes Gutenberg made major improvements to the Asian printing press in the 1440s, and its use spread to hundreds of European cities. "By 1500, there were 1700 presses at work in a total of 300 towns."[77]

Then the Chinese fleets were grounded in 1430, by an emperor determined to keep his subjects isolated and in ignorance,[78] Western mariners had the oceans to themselves. Magellan, Vasco da Gama, and their crews explored the coasts of Africa and gained a new route to the Indies, and in 1492 Christopher Columbus discovered the Americas. Within another fifty years, the Europeans had settlements all around the world.

It was another case of the West winning by default. With its fifty-year head start, the Chinese might have been the people who settled Australia, New Zealand, North and South America, and Africa. One might surmise that Europe didn't so much win, but that the others lost; and they lost because their elites were truly parasitic, hogging all the goodies for themselves and giving nothing to their unhappy subjects. It's a tale as old as time; the elites held back progress for thousands of years just as they still do in half the nations of the world.

There lies the explanation for the Rise of the West: Western people did it, yes; but they had help. The rulers in Asia, Africa, and the Middle East, by obstructing their own people, holding them in servitude, left the field open to Europeans. For those who worry whether Europeans succeeded by being more capable than other people, there lies the answer: Europeans won by default, the fault of the dominating elites around the world. Think of it this way: I can barely run, but I could win the Boston Marathon if nobody else was allowed to run and they gave me 1,000 years to finish!

Although Europeans had gained educational and technical superiority by 1500, they were at constant risk of being invaded and occupied by Muslim forces. However, in 1571, after the Ottoman forces invaded Cyprus and entered the Adriatic Sea to attack Venice, the Muslim fleet suffered a major defeat at the battle of Lepanto. Hundreds of Turkish galleys were sunk, and their commander fled. The allied Venetians and Spanish turned back the assault and liberated 15,000 enslaved Christians, (most of them chained as galley slaves), ending Muslim attacks from their Eastern strongholds. But the Ottoman threat continued on land, where they had conquered most of Eastern Europe, and were still intent on occupying Austria.

Then, in 1683, there was another turning point: Technical advances in weaponry, along with the Polish cavalry, helped the

Europeans halt the Muslim forces at the Gates of Vienna. After that, the Ottomans were gradually driven back from most of Eastern Europe. A sea change in useful knowledge had required 500 years to take place, but by the seventeenth century, the Europeans were far ahead of the Islamic and Asian people, and the sun never set on their ships exploring the world's oceans.

A FEW TURNING POINTS IN HISTORY: OPENING MINDS VERSUS CLOSING MINDS

After 1100 AD, the future course of nations was heavily determined by several decisive turning points: In the twelfth century, leaders in Muslim nations supported their conservative imam, Al Ghazali, not the more liberal thinker, Averroes, thereby tightening their theocratic autocracy and closing the minds of their people. In the fifteenth century the Chinese emperor scuttled his navy, ending trade and exploration, isolating his people, and leaving the world's oceans open to Europeans. In the sixteenth century Martin Luther provoked new religious and scientific thought; adaptations to the printing press spread literacy and learning throughout Europe, and the victory at Lepanto blocked the invasion of Italy by the Muslims. In the seventeenth century, advances in weaponry helped the Europeans turn back the Muslim forces besieging Vienna; and freedom-seeking Europeans were emigrating to the Americas, Australia, Canada, and New Zealand.

By 1675, after the Glorious Revolution added to the freedom of the English people, and its emigres were building a new industrial colossus in North America, the superior power and technology of Western civilization had been firmly established. The European people had turned back the Muslim threat from outside and rejected the internal straitjackets that the elites were so desperately trying to keep in place.

The huge advances in physical science and technical knowledge armed the European explorers with overwhelming military supremacy. Before long, English steam-powered gunships and well-armed troops could roam the great rivers of China and the teeming cities of India, gaining control of their ports and access to their economies. American clipper ships would race from New England harbors to the Far East and back, filled with cargoes of new and rare commodities. Modern technology had blossomed and its technicians and innovators were being born and raised by the families scattered within the relatively free nations of Europe and America.

THE POWER OF FREE ECONOMIES

"What makes me an optimist is that tens of thousands of scientists and entrepreneurs are right now hard at work trying to develop brand-new energy sources...they think they know how to bring power to people, and at least one of them is probably right."

JOHAN NORBERG
HTTP://WWW.JOHANNORBERG.NET/.

HOW MECHANICS, CARPENTERS, AND ENGINEERS CREATED THE INDUSTRIAL REVOLUTION

A nation now needed a great source of inventors, and the unique qualities of such mechanically gifted and imaginative minds had to be found in the varied ranks of the great masses of ordinary people.

Samuel Smiles observed in his survey of the engineers and emerging scientists that built the Industrial Revolution in England that they mostly came from rural farm families where the youth were apprenticed out into practical trades at a young age:

> "All the early engineers were self-taught in their profession…brought up mostly in remote country places…. But genius is of no locality, and springs alike from the farmhouse, the peasant's hut, or the herd's shieling…. Strange, indeed, it is that the men who built our bridges, docks, lighthouses, canals, and railways, should nearly all have been country-bred boys."[79]

Those boys became available because of a relatively open society with opportunities for young, hard-working tradesmen. Smiles tells us:

> "Our engineers may be regarded as the makers of modern civilization. The problems of political history cannot properly be interpreted without reference to the people themselves—how they lived and how they worked and what they did to promote the civilization of the nation…. Are not the men who have made the motive power of the country, and immensely increased its productive strength, the men *above all others* who have tended to make the country what it is?"[80]

Italics added to concede that Samuel Smiles scooped this author on the "totally new" concept that it was the ordinary people, like mechanics and engineers, "above all others," who built modern industry and thus the booming economies of today. By 1600 the extra freedom enjoyed by Europeans provided them with the genius of tens of thousands of their common people, an advantage that the more oppressive nations of the world could never enjoy. "The new printing presses were spewing out over 2,000 titles every year by 1600 and by 1815 that had risen to about 20,000 annually.... Cheap stores of technical knowledge moved outwards to the men of action and affairs, the military, the administration, the landowners."[81]

Meanwhile, the autocratic rulers of Asia and the Middle East restricted the use of printing, fearing their subjects might find out what was happening outside their closed society. "The literacy gap between Europe and Turkey was the difference between fifty percent and five percent, a tenfold difference, while the difference between publication rates was a factor of ten thousand."[82]

Once technology became vital to a nation's success, and its creative source only available from the masses of common people, Western civilization had gained an additional edge. Educated, free, and literate people became essential natural resources. and the greatest benefits for both the population and their nation arose where a broad segment of the people was included in the economic activity of their community. The people of the West kept accumulating useful knowledge and technical skills because they were able to. Elsewhere, the people were chained by the domineering elites. That unique differential, where many citizens had the opportunity to think and act purposefully, expanded rapidly around 300 years ago, and gained additional momentum for the European people.

In just the last 100 years we have seen the advance from horse drawn buggies, to automobiles, to airplanes, intercontinental rockets, and spaceships. That steady progress has always been fed by, 1) the accumulation of knowledge and, 2) its application to practical uses. Throughout history, those advances, applications, and utilizations of a growing body of knowledge occurred most significantly from the efforts of free people.

The rapid spread, adaptations, and improvements made to such radical innovations as the printing press was not an achievement of the "West" or some kind of "cultural force." Beginning in the 1400s, it was the ordinary workers in hundreds of small European towns who built, improved, and operated the presses. They were enabled by their freedom, motivated by self-interest, and they were rewarded by being able to keep the fruit of their labor. This rather clear record—that free and informed people are essential to build a great nation—has been consistently seen in the historic examples of all nations on earth but is still the subject of heated debate among the experts. Why, we must ask, is something so clear debated so feverishly? Hint: the independent, creative, and enterprising individual human being is the elite's worst nightmare; they find it rather difficult to control such a feisty yet productive person.

The importance of that feisty yet productive individual had long been recognized in ancient Greece, Rome, and the Renaissance cities of Europe. The heroic nature of the individual had first been glorified almost 3,000 years ago in Homer's epics about the Fall of Troy, the magnificence of Ulysses, and the subsequent adventures of Odysseus on his long journey back home. Such heroic figures reached a new height more than 2,000 years later in 1494 when the citizens of Florence re-established their Republic. To celebrate their freedom, they commissioned a young artist to create a gigantic and heroic figure of David, the legendary tyrant killer. Kenneth Clark has vividly described that statue's significance:

> Michelangelo's creation "is vast, defiant and nude.... When we come to the head, we are aware of a spiritual force that the ancient world never knew.... It involves a contempt for convenience and a sacrifice of all those pleasures that contribute to what we call civilized life....

And yet we recognize that to despise material obstacles, and even to defy the blind forces of fate, is man's supreme achievement; and since, in the end, civilization depends on man extending his powers of mind and spirit to the utmost, we must reckon the emergence of Michelangelo as one of the great events of western man."[83]

That elevation of man as a sacred individual, endowed with certain rights and deserving of respect, found fertile soil in Christian societies. That Christian message of compassion and concern for the poorest among us was underscored in John Steinbeck's classic novel *The Grapes of Wrath*. His readers cannot help but empathize with the plight of the migrants, leaving the dust bowl of Oklahoma in the 1920's and 1930's, to go west and build new lives in California. In that classic novel, Jim Casy advocates the belief that every man comes from a Divine source and therefore possesses a holiness or divinity that entitles each human to equal rights, respect, and justice—that every human is a "David."

Steinbeck was echoing Carl Sandberg's poem, "We are the people," when in chapter XX he writes Ma Joad's words, "Why, Tom, we're the people that live. They ain't gonna wipe us out. Why we're the people--we go on." That message honoring the common people is also similar to Emerson's position supporting the natural laws of justice that are provided for every person by a truly democratic state.

It is unfortunate that, while many people do persist, they have had to struggle mightily just "to go on." But Christian nations are unique in that their sustaining creed has helped ordinary people achieve many victories in the laboratory of history. Whether one likes religious faiths or not, it must be acknowledged that the cultural observance of compassion and forgiveness has helped Christian nations. Thomas Cahill explains (in "How the Irish Saved Civilization") that when St. Patrick visited Ireland in the fifth-century, he freed those people from the need to sacrifice their children on stone altars to appease vengeful gods: "Christ had died once for all… Yes, the Irish would have said, here's a story that answers our deepest needs…It is our lives not our deaths, that this God wants." In this way, Christianity offered a rock-solid foundation, freed from fear, dedicated to human action—a new-found confidence and independence on which a revitalized Western civilization could be built.

Historians have sought to chart such extraordinary milestones ever since Herodotus and Thucydides of ancient Greece and Rome wrote the earliest histories of man's exploits. In 2007, distinguished English historian John Burrow published his monumental analysis describing the work of hundreds of those historians. However, after 485 pages he writes, "This book can have no conclusions: the study and writing of history is still going on… We do have the advantage of hindsight, but historians have learned to be wary of overexploiting this."[84]

Nevertheless, Burrow observed that "the greatest flowering of genius occurred when the reins of government were loosest, and a populace was free to find ways to overcome both fate and material obstacles."[85] Doesn't that sounds like a slightly veiled conclusion matching the one presented in this book?

Although Burrow claimed to draw no conclusions from his work, he did hint at the possibility of gaining conclusions from the study of past human activity: "world history, being essentially comparative and concerned with, in Braudel's phrase, *la longue durée*, needs large-scale organizing categories which are not distinctly national or specific to a narrowly defined period."[86] He also indicated the value of micro-history when studied as a case analysis of actual small societies and how they functioned. Such studies, he explains, "are research driven, rather than theory-driven…they can form not a conclusion or climax, but a suitable kind of coda…it illuminates something more general than itself but is not necessarily to be thought of as 'evidence,' a brick to be added to an edifice of generalization built on the accumulation of cases, though in principle it could eventually be used in this way."[87]

Apparently, Burrow was not inclined to draw conclusions himself from history's many cases of successful nations but did recognize that conclusions could be made based on an accumulation of evidence and events, "or a sequence of them." In this book we have relied on just such cases of actual governmental experiences; they serve as evidence based on historical research, not theory; and we have found that those many "bricks" assembled do lead to useful generalizations.

Perhaps Burrow did not want to go the final step, and antagonize the powers that be, but he did set up a framework for this author: Case studies of the past, combined with an accumulation of evidence, based on historical research, not theory, can be assembled into useful generalizations: Free people achieve more than enslaved people; they create superior economies and provide a higher standard of living for their people.

SUMMARY

Although the "science" of government cannot be reduced to absolute mathematical certainties, there are a few principles that have been helpful to all communities for thousands of years. If country-bred boys created the machines that powered the Industrial Revolution, and such individuals are the essential source of societal advances, it follows that free communities have an advantage over oppressed communities. Only the former unleashes the enormous energy and imagination of a multitude of involved and motivated people.

Because that fact relegates elites to mere observers and critics, the elites have always had to find a way to conceal the importance of the masses of people who actually make successful nations blossom. In democracies, where ruthless force must be minimized, the elites have found it useful to make both economics and political history extremely complicated, because that justifies their role as essential managers at the highest levels of government.

The truth is that the great advances of Western civilization came from the hard scientists and all the mechanics, engineers, farmers, and tradesmen who pioneered the technical and scientific discoveries and innovations that made life easier and our work more productive. In the next chapter we will see how Europeans found "the secret weapon" to power that advance—by separating Science from Religion, they unleashed the physical scientists, engineers, and mechanics to create extraordinary technical progress.

CHAPTER 7-

The Secret Weapon of the West: Separating Religion and Science

 "Western civilization… stands by two great heritages. One is the scientific spirit of adventure… humility of the intellect. The other great heritage is Christian ethics… humility of the spirit. These two heritages are logically, thoroughly consistent."
~~ Richard P. Feynman

$\mathbf{F}$OR THOSE OF US BROUGHT up and educated in families and communities that were shaped by a love of freedom and a deep respect for individual rights, it may seem surprising that so many other people throughout the world have accepted a subordinate status. It is perhaps a testament to the power of their haughty elites that those people didn't even know what they were missing. James A. Michener's book *Poland* illustrates how, even in Europe just a few centuries ago, many peasants meekly accepted a status where they were rarely able to eat meat or take a day off from their labors. Generations of people in many countries have been trained, like dogs, to accept such an unhappy role–and that was done because their elites like it that way!

Fortunately, there was a current of freedom that existed and kept finding expression, as reviewed in Chapters Three and Five. Around 1000AD there was a widespread revival in Europe of both democratic traditions and scientific studies. The movement was led by the Franciscan and Dominican monks who established universities for the study of accumulated prior learning. The Catholic Church was not as rigid as most religions, and its role benefitted from its hierarchies, with bishops at the top, followed by priests, with lowly monks at the bottom. As we often see in history, progress came mostly from the bottom. It was the Catholic monks, the studious teachers in those monasteries and universities, that initiated the study of the physical sciences. (It was "only" the bishops on top that wanted to burn such rebels at the stake).

Relying on strict logic, the monks' reasoning developed inevitably into separating the physical sciences from spiritual beliefs. Nothing like that was allowed anywhere else on earth. As early as the twelfth and thirteenth century AD, there were stirrings of free thinking throughout Europe. Marsiglio of Padua (1275-1342) wrote *Defensor Pacis*, a treatise that helped advance representative government. Written 400 years after the formation of Iceland's parliament, the Althing, and a century after the Magna Carta, these "democratic" principles became part of the literature documenting the striving of the common people of Europe for more liberty.

Marsiglio was a friend of William of Ockham (1285–1347), one of the Oxford University-based Franciscan friars who were challenging the pope's positions on faith and property. The two men advanced the proposition that "ultimate sovereignty resides in the majority of the people.... General Councils are to be formed by popular election.... Councils alone should lay down standards of orthodoxy, and the Church is not to meddle in affairs of State."[88] And those principles were not new; Venice had lived by them for 700 years before Marsiglio was born.

ORIGIN OF THE KISS RULE AND OCCAM'S RAZOR

"With all things being equal, the simplest explanation tends to be the right one."

WILLIAM OF OCKHAM B.1285AD.
(KEEP IT SIMPLE, STUPID, 2005AD

As early as the 1200s, such pioneering teachers as Albert the Great and Robert Grosseteste were working at universities in Paris, Cologne, Milan, and Cambridge, passing on their ideas about scientific inquiry, observation, and experimental methods to students such as Roger Bacon and Thomas Aquinas. These members of the Catholic Church advanced the physical sciences and the separation of church and state, sowing the seeds for the Reformation to come a couple hundred years later. For their efforts, both Marsiglio and Ockham were excommunicated in 1328 and barely escaped from Avignon to find protection in Munich under Emperor Louis.[89]

The salient point is not that the West offered the perfect conditions for advances, but that its elites' resistance to advances by the common people was not as absolute or destructive as everywhere else! Less suppression means a tad more freedom. A little freedom means a lot!

It is true that all religions have had a downside; just like elites and governments, they have imposed a certain degree of stifling conformity and oppression. However, some have helped people more and done less harm than others. Seven hundred years after Thomas Aquinas was born, and nineteen hundred years after Jesus Christ was born,

Bishop Desmond Tutu and Reverend Martin Luther King were still spreading the Christian message of Compassion and Love when they marched for racial equality. Many other Christians have joined such peaceful marches to gain equal rights for what Mahatma Gandhi calls "the poorest among us." Perhaps, just as for governments and rulers, religions that have done more good than harm are to be treasured.

Bishop Tutu always wore his cassock and carried a Bible and a Christian Cross when he spoke in public for Equal Rights.

By 1500AD, there were universities in all the major European cities. At the same time, the widespread use of printing presses had increased public literacy and helped the people of Europe understand the new technologies as well as the logic for political and economic freedom. Religious leaders in all other regions of the world suppressed such learning; the Christian monks advanced learning, a differential tipping point that illustrates the valuable contribution of Christianity to Europe's success.

The big pay-off from these universities and the new ways of thinking that they nurtured, appeared suddenly in 1517 when Martin Luther, a very humble and lowly monk, in a small, lonely parish, famously posted his ninety-five "complaints" to the monastery's door for all the world to read. He listed the faults that he saw in Church dogma. Then, to add fuel to the fire, he claimed that a devout individual could direct his prayers directly to his personal God without the intervention of priests. European royalty and the pope would never again have the power they had exerted for centuries. Luther was one of the obscure but persistent little guys who made things happen!

THE ADVANCE OF LEARNING AND LITERACY IN EUROPE

The Protestant Revolution unleashed the genie from the bottle; if God was supreme, and people could worship Him directly without the rituals of a priestly class, then kings and priests became mere humans. The Divine Right of Kings was unmasked and gradually became a historical artifact! Thus, ancient ideas supporting scientific inquiry were revitalized in Europe as early as the thirteenth and fourteenth centuries. And that liberation of thinking and doing helped England eventually become the center of the "Industrial Revolution." The spread of knowledge, combined with the separation of religion and science, supported the subsequent progress of the West. Once science was freed from religious dogma, technology took off, and the rest is history!

The long and slow advance of technology gathered speed in the seventeenth and eighteenth centuries. "The English empirical tradition proved particularly hospitable to such an outlook: such men as Francis Bacon (d.1626) and the founders of the Royal Society (1660) looked forward with complete confidence to the benefits they expected to arise from technical improvements arrived at through careful observation and experiment."[90] It was that open and inquisitive environment which allowed common mechanics and engineers to invent the machines that powered the Industrial Revolution in England.

The Muslim nations were held back by their theocratic rulers who outlawed the pursuit of physical science. The Muslim priests did not appreciate their own famed Muslim scholar in Spain who was promoting ideas on personal liberty and scientific inquiry, so Averroes was exiled, and a curtain drawn over the minds of the Muslim people. "The net result of this intellectual evolution was to throttle almost all innovation in Moslem science and philosophy."[91]

A similar closing of minds occurred in China in 1400, when its Admiral Cheng Ho was ordered to return his fleets to China. The Chinese elite wanted no foreign influences corrupting their absolute rule over a peasant society, and so the curtain came down there, as it had in the Muslim nations.[92] The great religions of Asia also taught a relatively submissive philosophy, calling for an acceptance of fate and discouraging human activism. The Christian message was more inspiring and the teachers in those early universities had little sympathy for a passivity in earthly matters.

A simple pastor, John Knox, epitomized the vitality of the Protestant movement. In 1559, when he began preaching the new Protestantism to a receptive people in Scotland, Knox's message was taken up by George Buchanan who had also been educated at the University of St. Andrews. Together, they argued that political power belonged to all people, not to kings or their lords and ladies. Note that their doctrine, advocating the pollical sovereignty of the people, was put in place 100 years before a similar message was written about by John Locke!

Moreover, Buchanan went further than Locke in explaining the fundamental right of citizens to overthrow their leaders. As Arthur Herman reports in his book *How the Scots Invented the Modern World*, Buchanan argued that when a ruler failed to act in the people's interest, then the citizens have the right to remove that tyrant, "even to the point of killing him." Buchanan's book, *The Law of Government Among the Scots*, presenting these new ideas about the nature of political authority, was published in 1579, two years before the Dutch people became united to overthrow their leaders as justified by their *Oath of Abjuration*. And John Calvin, born four years after John Knox, led the Reformation in Switzerland. Clearly, we must credit Martin Luther with creating such widespread demands for religious and political liberty, all eloquently set forth in the 16th century, long before the Enlightenment philosophers picked up the idea.

This unique boost, that was to help Europeans move ahead of all other parts of the world, was the work of a series of persistent individuals who believed passionately in two new principles: 1) that governments are formed by the people and for the people—not for the rulers, and 2) that spiritual beliefs are based on faith and not subject to proof, whereas science, dealing with the physical world, can be understood and used to better man's well-being. Some of those European rebels were condemned by the kings and priests, made to retract their public statements, or exiled, and often simply burned at the stake. However, many persisted and both freedom and science began to flourish. It could have happened anywhere: Calcutta, Timbuctoo, Moscow, or Cairo. But the political and religious elites in those places ruthlessly blocked such new ways of thinking. Even in Europe it had been a long slow slog to achieve free and innovative thinking.

SUMMARY

The European people owe much to the original Judeo-Greek people's elevation of man as a heroic and sacred figure. That unique legacy helped the Europeans forge an extraordinary progression of both freedom and knowledge from 1000–1750 AD. It was the combination of, universities, separating science from religion, a bit of personal freedom, and the resulting technological advances that gradually powered the Industrial Revolution. Unforgettably, those success stories were only won by the continuous demands of our liberty-loving ancestors who, most readers will now understand, had very little help from their rulers.

It is worth noting that even today most of those efforts by common people are ignored by the academics who teach our children that it was the Enlightenment philosophers who created the advance of democratic governance. Taking that credit away from the common people may not amount to an evil "conspiracy," because a natural disdain for both religion and the common people may motivate academics to credit intellectuals like themselves for the advance of free nations. However, John Knox was no intellectual. He was born in 1505 and attended his local school before going to St. Andrews and becoming a priest in the Roman Catholic Church. At one point he was captured by French pirates and served as a chained slave in their galleys. After escaping, he returned to Scotland and worked tirelessly as a minister bringing the ennobling messages of Christianity and free government to the Scottish people.

St. Patrick, who brought Christianity to Ireland had a similar background. As did Martin Luther himself. And it was the humble Puritans and Quakers who not only led the demand for liberty in England and its colonies, but also added their strength to the call to end, first the slave trade, and then, the institution of slavery itself. Thus, it was many such common individuals who advanced both faith and freedom, science, and prosperity. It was part of the ageless struggle of ordinary people against their elites, gaining liberty one tiny crumb at a time.

In the next chapter we will see how many similar settlors brought their Christian Faith, and their search for liberty and opportunity, to start-up what became the most prosperous and freest country in history. And, the reader will discover, they did it with virtually no government help.

CHAPTER 8-

America's Example—How to Start Up a Democracy

"'Keep, ancient lands, your storied pomp,'
cries she with silent lips.
'Give me your tired, your poor, your huddled
masses yearning to breathe free…'"
Emma Lazarus' words carved on the Statue of Liberty

U P TO THIS POINT, WE have looked back through recorded history, pausing briefly to examine the major steppingstones of progress—those isolated and rare communities of people who found sufficient freedom to build open and dynamic societies. That string of start-ups began in the Middle East in Judea and Phoenicia, moved to southern Europe with the ancient Greeks and Romans, and then gradually spread throughout much of Western Europe.

The exciting future of the European people was presaged during the Italian Renaissance, which from 1200–1500 displayed a rebirth of art, knowledge, and scientific inquiry. After 1500, following the Reformation, scientific advances accelerated, the demand for basic human rights intensified, and by the 1630s there was a flood of the most persistent pioneers of liberty leaving their homes in northwestern Europe to take their ideas of freedom and human dignity across the Atlantic Ocean to settle the New World of America.

The American pioneers, aware of history's record of free societies, and with an understanding of the governing mechanics of prior free republics, were soon able to build a colossus—a country exemplifying all that was good from prior republics and then some! Anyone aware of the obstacles that had been overcome for mankind to finally arrive at the American success story must not only stand in awe of those advances but should also be doubly motivated not to let it all slip away. If Americans do not want to lose their unique homeland, it is essential to fully understand what caused this country's people to enjoy more liberty and prosperity than any other people in history.

START-UP SOCIETIES MUST FIRST BE SETTLED: IMMIGRANTS COME LATER

In 2004, when seeking to describe the nature of American culture, Samuel P. Huntington explained that first he had to expose the partial truths and half-truths that have come to obscure an understanding of our nation's origins: "Current thinking of our past is based on two propositions that are true but only partially true and yet often accepted as the whole truth."[93] These claims are first that America is a nation of immigrants and second that America's founding principles are identified by a set of political beliefs, the America Creed. "Neither one of these is the whole truth concerning America.... They tell us nothing about the society that attracted the immigrants or the culture that produced the Creed."

In fact, Huntington writes, "America is a founded society created by seventeenth and eighteenth-century settlers, almost all of whom came from the British Isles. Their values, and their prior institutions and culture, provided the foundation for what was to drive the new nation. It was those early settlers' beliefs and customs that substantially shaped all the developments in the following centuries."[94]

Thus, the truth is that the nation was founded by people from three northern European nations. One hundred and forty years later, in 1760, when those settlers and their descendants agreed that a separation from the English sovereign was essential, there were 2.5 million people in the colonies excluding slaves. Eighty-five percent were from the British Isles and 13 percent from Germany and Holland. Thus, 98 percent were from those three countries. They were the people who built America during its first 140 years, from 1620 to 1760. They were united by a desire to guarantee their personal liberty and gain economic opportunity. Even before the 1775 revolt, these settlers had gained representative assemblies in each state.

The earliest settlers in Virginia and Massachusetts did have to make compromises to get here. The opportunity many were offered was to come over as part of a corporate venture, pledged to contribute to the company some of the goods they were to produce in return for free passage. But human nature being what it is, after landing on these shores, their motivation to produce anything was weak, knowing it would go into the company stores. Those that were subject to such forced sharing of whatever they produced, did little. (It was another illustration of one of the fatal weaknesses in communal, or socialist sharing). The English owners, soon seeing nothing happening, and unable to sell land to settlers, soon gave up their plans and "each male settler was granted fifty acres of land for each member of his family."[95]

Once granted the essential right to work their own land and keep the product of their toil, the settlers worked hard, motivated by the ingrained self-interest that has always and will probably always motivate Homo sapiens to their ultimate effort. The futile idea that we all should share equally may be profoundly satisfying to us on a moral basis but must be recognized as a dangerous delusion that has proven in practice to mean there is less for everyone. For those who seek a socialist America, history shows that it has already been tried and was abandoned within a few years! Been there, done that!

The early settlers of American colonies were fully aware of the intent of elites to gain advantages for themselves by establishing preferential laws and institutions. There was little opportunity to do so in the northern colonies, but the South was infected by more aristocratic overseers such as Lord Baltimore. "In 1632, ten million acres of land on the upper Chesapeake Bay were granted by the English king Charles I to Cecilius Calvert, Lord Baltimore."[96] The king provided a charter for that grant that gave Lord Baltimore total freedom to enact whatever laws and institutions for said lands as he alone wished. That good Lord accordingly drew up a detailed plan to recreate an English manorial society, with plots of thousands of acres, each to be run by lords, who would recruit tenants to work the land and pay rents to the privileged elites above them.

A similar plan was attempted in 1663 with the founding of Carolina by eight proprietors, including Sir Anthony Asley-Cooper. The latter aristocrat, fully enjoying his grant from the king, employed one John Locke, the noted philosopher, as his secretary. Together they "formulated the Fundamental Constitutions of Carolina. This document, like the Charter of Maryland before it, provided a blueprint for an elite hierarchical society based on control by a landed elite."[97] John Locke did famously write about allowing the people some rights, but he never advocated real liberty for them, and as Cooper's secretary he appears to have approved of "a landed elite."

In all these cases the plans of the elites failed because the settlers, all being of very independent spirit, refused to cooperate; they simply went elsewhere in the vast new lands of the American wilderness. By the 1720s the settlers' refusal to submit induced the king to withdraw the powers of his appointed lords, and the colonies were allowed to establish general assemblies that granted a vote to all propertied male citizens. It was the members of those assemblies about 50 years later who got together and declared total independence from the king and his aristocrats. They just would not accept half measures.

ONE TABLESPOON OF LITERATE, HONEST PEOPLE

The original American settlers faced an empty wilderness, a desolation that required them to start from scratch, plow new land, and wait decades to add a few tools or draft animals to help in their labor. But they also had a few great advantages that enhanced their chances for success in creating a mighty new nation. They were products of their parents' and grandparents' past centuries of struggle in north-western Europe to obtain freedom. Like Isaac Newton, the settlers could see far because they stood on the shoulders of the giants who had paved the way before them. They knew all about the political gains that had been very slowly gained in England and Holland by their ancestors. The settlers heading to America wanted all that and more!

For the English and Scots, it had been 400 years of struggle, insurrections, and riots to extract small concessions from the aristocratic elite that ruled their homeland. The minor aristocrats in England had gained a bit of liberty way back in 1215 when they prevailed on King John to sign the Magna Carta. By 1600, the ordinary people had also gradually eked out small tidbits of freedom and rights for themselves. But those concessions, more than had ever been gained by most other people throughout the world, were not enough. Those independent and impatient citizens could see the chance for real freedom in the New World.

Consequently, there was a great flood of people sailing out of their homelands in the early- to mid-1600s intent on finding a full measure of freedom. These people were not a group to be trifled with, and within 150 years would take up arms and gain total control of the colony they had settled in.

ADD A DASH OF PROVEN INSTITUTIONS FOR A HEAD START

Like the people of most "start-up" nations, the American settlers benefitted from a combination of strong cultural roots, a vigorous self-reliant population, and a thorough experience with benign and enabling laws and institutions. Their ancestors in Europe had gained a taste of representative government and the right to trial by jury with an accessible financial system that permitted secure ownership of property.

Armed with that awareness of freedom's enabling institutions, and suddenly finding themselves unhindered by the burdens of an established elite, their communities flourished. There have been few cases in history where the keys to national success have been more clearly demonstrated. The settlers of North America had unity, drive, and a demanding but uplifting faith, plus knowledge of democratic institutions and the mechanics of open economies. And they were free to act—safe from invading nations from the outside, and free of oppressive elites on the inside.

Clearly, the American settlers were a unique group that left three Northern European nations, over a 130-year period, from 1620 to 1750, bringing their advanced ideas on freedom, useful institutions, and the rule of law with them. They were, in Louis Hartz's words, a "fragment," a breakout group escaping their past countries, split off, but carrying a positive existing culture and empowering beliefs. And, perhaps most important, they escaped the elites who were still using every device possible to limit the opportunity and liberty of their subjects.

Ben Franklin looked back to ancient republics and cherry-picked their best features to help the Founders design the American Constitution.

Thus, the great battles for more freedom in Europe leading up to the seventeenth century, which were never fully successful, did get satisfactorily resolved, at least for the new settlers, who just decided to leave that all behind and sail to the New World. Their freedom "was resolved not through revolt or fabulous constitutional invention, but through migration, through leaving the 'old world' behind."[98] They simply sailed away, escaping all elites and the rigid class structure that had been stifling their liberty and opportunity.

Hartz points out that the extensive political knowledge of the settlers, and their desire for liberty under a very limited government, ensured a smooth transition to a sound Republican form of government: "Some Americans feared a military dictatorship, and some feared a monarchy. In fact, both were ruled out by the historic character of the American fragment. An army was needed to liquidate British rule, but it was not needed for any other purpose. Monarchy was eliminated, but it too was not needed, there could be no need for a 'restoration.'"[99]

Hartz's point is that America was blessed by the background of its settlers: "Of course, all fragment cultures are by definition distinctively homogeneous."[100] And what helped even more was the fact that "Republican virtue was insured by a cultural heritage out of the past, ultimately out of the first of the seventeenth century migrations. It was this heritage that had given them a tempered Enlightenment, a traditionalistic revolution, ultimately a successful republican constitution."[101]

Huntington echoes these comments by Hartz: "Settlers leave an existing society, usually in a group, in order to create a new community, a city on a hill, in a new and often distant territory. They are imbued with a sense of collective purpose. Implicitly or explicitly, they subscribe to a compact or charter that defines the basis of the community they create.... Immigrants, in contrast, do not create a new society. They move from one society to a different society.... They come later because they wanted to become part of the society that the settlers had created.... Before immigrants could come to America, settlers had to found America.... The term 'immigrant' came into the English language in the 1780s to distinguish current arrivals from the founding settlers."[102]

Because the settlers placed their "cultural stamp" on America, in Wilbur Zelinsky's words, they established the principles of the American people for centuries, determining the social and cultural geography of the nation. A defining characteristic of these settlers was a deep distrust of elites, aristocracies, experts, and government regulations. Zelinsky calls this phenomenon "The Doctrine of First Effective Settlement,"[103] and it was those original principles that shaped America for the first 300 years when it grew rapidly to world supremacy.

THE NINETEENTH CENTURY: FORGING PROGRESS AND FORCING REFORM

By the end of the 1800s, almost 300 years after the first settlements, the American population had broadened to include immigrants from most European nations. These new arrivals had heard what the settlers had accomplished, what they had gained in freedom and prosperity, how most of them owned the land they lived on, and, most importantly, how here in the New World a person could be the master of his own destiny.

Those subsequent European immigrants, after joining the massive number of descendants of the original settlers, eagerly assumed the new ways and culture of America, forming a patriotic and unified people that had by 1900 established the United States as the strongest arsenal of freedom and prosperity that the world had ever seen. And, while those people were doing all that, they tended to some major reforms in government.

America's industrial might was cobbled together by giants in finance and industry but was powered by the workers at the bottom. The "Robber Barons" like Rockefeller, Carnegie, Vanderbilt, and Morgan created some of the world's largest business enterprises and earned extraordinary personal fortunes, but there was bound to be problems of equity. Reforms were needed and political leaders began to act in the mid-to-late-1800s. First slavery was outlawed and the former slaves given the vote. Second, they broke up the monopolies and limited unfair trade practices. Third, Samuel Gompers founded the American Federation of Labor (AFL) in 1886 to protect the nation's working men and women. At its pinnacle, the AFL had approximately 1.4 million members and is credited with successfully negotiating wage increases for its members and enhancing workplace safety.

The Sherman Antitrust Act was passed almost unanimously by Congress in 1890. It was aimed at curtailing a major fault of unrestrained capitalism—the monopolistic practices that limited competition. Presidents Taft and Roosevelt used Senator Sherman's anti-monopoly law in the late 1800s and early 1900s to prosecute dozens of violators and break up the offending corporate interests. "Buck" Duke was a prime example, consolidating the tobacco industry by whatever means necessary. Jim Rumford succinctly writes, "Men like Duke weren't satisfied with a piece of the profit pie. They wanted the entire pie."[104] (Just like the lion in Aesop's fable!)

REFORMING CAPITALISM

"If we will not endure a king as a political power, we should not endure a king over the production, transportation, and sale of any of the necessaries of life."

~~~ SENATOR JOHN SHERMAN
SHERMAN ANTITRUST ACT - 1890

Clearly, not all the politicians were in bed with the Robber Barons, so the problem was mitigated but not fully solved. The titans in the financial sector were not to be shackled. In chapter eleven, we will see how a few wealthy financiers managed to get the government to establish the Federal Reserve Bank. In spite of the Trust Busters work, the wealthiest financial elites continued to plot how to gain a stranglehold on our economic affairs.

However, reformers did find ways to reduce the conflict between labor and management and addressed major social and political problems. The Civil War was endured, the Southern plantation life disrupted, and slavery was abolished. The abolitionist and suffragette movements were led primarily by middle-class whites in the Northern states, many inspired by their religious faith. Both movements were to succeed but had to overcome opposition from Congress and most of the establishment in Washington.

The Civil War freed the country of slavery and in 1870 the Fifteenth Amendment to the Constitution gave the vote to all male citizens. However, Jim Crow laws, enacted by Democratic-controlled state legislatures in the South, limited the rights of blacks for another 100 years. Finally, over three decades, in the 1940-60s, it took over a dozen court cases, executive orders, and Constitutional Amendments to rid the country of the worst discriminatory evils. Under presidents Truman, Eisenhower, Kennedy, and Johnson, this process gradually ended segregation in the military, schools, voting booths, employment offices, and transportation.

A parallel movement to give women the right to vote had gotten its first success in the Territory of Wyoming in 1869. Then, in 1889, when Congress awarded Wyoming statehood, Congress reluctantly accepted that state's laws that included women as voters. In the 1890s, Colorado, Utah, and Idaho followed Wyoming's lead, and by 1918, seventeen states had given the vote to their women. Then, on January 1917, Alice Paul and the National Woman's Party (NWP) became the first people to ever picket the White House. Because of continuing opposition to a women's suffrage amendment, Paul and the other suffragists became more activist. They carried banners like "Mr. President How Long Must Women Wait for their Liberty?"

By 1919, women's suffrage had gained steam throughout the land. Alice Paul, a leader of the Suffragettes, led picketing groups, and parodied President Wilson's 1916 re-election slogan as "Wilson kept us out of Suffrage." The war effort and the beginning of a feminist movement had liberated the women, who in 1920, made up 25 percent of the labor force and were themselves a force not to be denied. President Wilson finally caved to the women's demands and the Nineteenth Constitutional Amendment was ratified in 1920.

The American people had not only forged the most prosperous nation on earth but in addition had forced major reforms to protect all its citizens. With all races and genders gaining the opportunity to participate in both democracy and a free economy, the Americans would engage in World War II under the leadership of its "Greatest Generation" to defeat two of the world's worst totalitarian regimes— Hitler's Nazi Germany and Hirohito's Imperial Japan. Most observers agreed that the victory won over those aggressor countries was due to the fact that America was enriched by the united efforts of everyone in the nation, each person contributing the best they could to a common desire to keep America free—*and* to help others remain free.

OPENING THE ECONOMY: ALLOWING EVERYONE THE OPPORTUNITY TO PARTICIPATE

The Americans' rapid rise to world supremacy was without parallel in history, virtually a miracle when compared to the destiny of all prior nations on earth. Never had so much been done, so quickly, by so few. Notably, that miracle had been achieved prior to World War I without a big government, without intellectuals or aristocracies, and with no income tax or a federal reserve bank. They did it by moving to a new location and creating laws and institutions guaranteeing their liberty. And they did it in record time because there were few elites suppressing their creative actions. In fact, the elites had kept a low profile for a couple hundred years until the likes of Paul Bunyan, Thomas Paine, Sam Houston, Davy Crockett, Sam Adams, "Stonewall" Jackson, and Abraham Lincoln were a distant memory.

The nation obviously benefitted from the ever-larger contributions coming from its people. The original population was continuously enriched by hordes of immigrants who came to share the freedom and opportunities available in America. Every adult got to vote, the economy was open to all, the government was small, foreign entanglements were avoided, and a moral and thrifty people took full advantage.

The bottom line, and perhaps the ultimate measure of a beneficial government, was that those Americans consistently raised the average standard of living for everyone in the nation.

"The federal government's Bureau of Economic Analysis—which is the source of consumption data for the United States—normally reports consumption for the entire nation.... Combined with World Bank data for the same year, these datasets show that the *poorest 20%* of Americans have higher average consumption per person than the averages for *all people* in most OECD nations, including the majority of its European members:"[105]

The same database showed that the average American had more disposable income than the people of every nation in the world. Even the economically bottom 20 percent of Americans have a higher standard of living than the *average* person in Sweden, Canada, Japan, Australia, Denmark, and Israel. There are only eleven nations in the world with more average disposable income than our bottom fifth, all European nations, and even those people enjoy only about 10 percent more buying power than America's poorest fifth.

"In 2010, the poorest 20% of Americans consumed three to 30 times more goods and services on average than the national averages for all people in an array of developing nations around the world."[106]

The success of the American people, and the nation they settled and organized, had accelerated for 300 years, and by 1910 they had surpassed all other nations in affluence, freedom, and independence. But the would-be elites were not to be resisted forever. During the last century, and especially since World War II, the nation's elites have become increasingly dominant in society, the schools, the government, and the many organizations that influence everything that happens in America.

THE CHRISTIAN SOLUTION

"Be behind Capitalism when Marxian Socialism would destroy private property and be behind Labor when Monopolistic Capitalism would claim the priority of profits over the right to a just wage."

~~FULTON J. SHEEN MARCH 2, 1943

More and more voters recognize the damage done by the elites but many blame America itself and its founding principles instead of recognizing the need to tame the elites. Criticisms of our country and its history currently include such "evils" as slavery, suppression of women, and the exploitation of factory workers—failings that had been substantially reformed by ordinary Americans more than half a century before these critics were born.

Today's elites encourage this misdirected blame game. They need to cover up the more important need to reform Wall Street and its financial shenanigans, the corruption that soils many office holders, the lobbying that buys privilege, and the uneven application of justice by our legal institutions. They have had to find new "reforms" to champion—currently reduced to arguing in favor of transgender bathrooms, free medical care for illegal immigrants, and safe rooms for those delicate souls offended by free speech.

But there is a method in their madness. Their intentions are neither charitable nor honorable. There is nothing new about elites. Throughout history their main objective has always been to rule over the common people. To gain control, the elites plan to keep reducing the individual American's liberty, strengthen their own grip on the levers of power, control what is taught in our public schools, and seduce more and more voters into silence and dependency.

SUMMARY

Why not agree that America, and the many other free nations of the past, have written the recipe for national success? Why not throw out the excuses about climate and geography? Why not admit that good institutions are easily designed, written, and established? Why not support the people of any nation who wish to set up such a system of effective government of the people, by the people, and exclusively for the people? Why tolerate all the despots cruelly dominating their people? As Howie Carr might exclaim, "How many more must die?" And above all, why let America's newest elites destroy all that has been accomplished and destroy the destination desired and admired by all the world's people?

If America is not to their liking, a failed state, why don't the critics pick a new home, a place that is preferable? The truth of the matter is that there is no "better" place for them to go to. Can you imagine them being happier in France, Saudi Arabia, Japan, Russia, Sweden, Venezuela, Vietnam, Brazil, China, Italy, or Uganda? Since it is obvious that there is no place they would prefer, why don't the critics admit that America is their number one choice and it therefore makes no sense to "totally transform" our country.

The solution to America's failings is not to radically change its institutions but to carefully adjust them so they work more for the people and less for the elites. Instead of rioting for relatively insignificant social issues, voters should be demanding an end to crony capitalism, banks too big to fail, foreign escapades that make no sense while killing and maiming our treasured youth, the abuses by greedy financial powers, the unjust tax system, and the corruption that infects our government and its ever-expanding agencies.

Because America's previous generations created the best place in the world to live, let us give praise where praise is due. Some modest tinkering is needed but let's abandon that "total transformation" baloney.

SUMMARY OF PART II

*Why Differing Levels of Freedom Explain How
Some People Achieved More Success Than Others*

*Case studies of history's past communities make it clear that
oppressed people, constantly enslaved to serve their masters, had
little opportunity to even think about the possibility of making
better things for better living.*

*Autocratic rulers limited technical and intellectual progress by
suppressing their people and even limited the use of what few innovations were developed, lest their subjects develop any idea of how
freedom could help them.*

*The few exceptions, where free nations originated, were founded
along the shores of the Mediterranean Sea by the Judean and
Phoenician people. Those experiments in self-government were
then advanced by the Greeks and Romans, who designed revolutionary new forms of constitutional government, and left a legacy
currently enjoyed by a growing number of free people in every
corner of the world.*

THE PARASITIC ROLE OF ELITES

PART III

Elites Escalate their War Against the People
(1750AD - 2000AD)

CHAPTER 9-

The False Lure of Socialism—Shaping the Children

 *We have no Government armed with Power capable of contending with human Passions unbridled by… morality and Religion…Our Constitution was made only for a moral and religious People. It is wholly inadequate to the government of any other.*

President John Adams

IT IS A GENERALLY WELL-ESTABLISHED fact that every attempt to establish socialist economies throughout history has failed. Will and Ariel Durant wrote a multi-volume *History of the World* and sought to draw lessons from their life's work: their chapter IX is titled "Socialism and History," and there they list dozens of socialist experiments over the last few millennia and explain how very few survived even 100 years.

Most of those attempts collapsed due to high taxes, corruption in the bureaucracy, and inefficiency in the economy. One example was when Chinese Emperor Wang An-shih imposed a government-run economy in 1050 AD. It shortly drew such criticism that he was deposed and his successor observed "that human corruptibility and incompetence make governmental control of industry impractical."[107]

What may come as a surprise to many Americans is that there are those among us who adore incompetency and corruption. Elites, unbound by moral scruples, dream constantly about ruling over a dumb incompetent public so they can revel in high levels of corruption at the top. That is not something new and should come as no surprise. For the last five thousand years elites have sought to keep their people ignorant and passive while they and their cronies feast of their nation's wealth.

The Durants cite all the factors that make free and fair economies work the best for their people but ask: "Why does history resound with protests and revolts against the abuses of industrial mastery, price manipulation, business chicanery, and irresponsible wealth. These abuses must be hoary with age, for there have been socialist experiments in a dozen countries and centuries."[108] That is an excellent question, and we have a perfect answer. But first, note the Durant's over-all conclusion regarding the Rise of nations:

"The character of natural resources and geography may offer opportunities, but only the imagination and initiative of leaders, and the hardy industry of followers, can transform the possibilities into fact; and only a similar combination can make a culture take form over a thousand natural obstacles. Man, not the earth, makes civilization."[109]

Thus, the Durants confirm that:

1. People can overcome most obstacles and they alone cause the success and failure of nations,

2. A free environment delivers the best for the people at large. BUT,

3. Once the elites corrupt capitalism, it works well for just those at the top. That is when some voters begin to hope for something better: a "socialist" economy.

With that third fact before us, can we understand socialism's appeal as an attractive alternative to capitalism? The Durants put their finger on the basic problem: "China, like other nations, was faced with a choice between private plunder and public graft." Several observations come to mind:

1. Unless you accept the fact that nothing dealing with people can ever be "perfect," you will always find fault with anything less than perfection. Unfortunately, our first choices often become picking the lesser evil, the least bad.

2. If our historians and economists agreed that ordinary people, when motivated and free, are essential to building a vibrant economy, the obvious impracticality of socialism would be made clear. Socialism involves the top-down control of the economy which then eliminates imaginative innovation, encourages corruption at the highest levels, reduces the freedom and motivation of the people, and prevents the efficiency and prosperity that comes from a free and competitive marketplace.

3. Part of socialism's appeal is that elites actively promote it because it provides them with comfy jobs at the top and gives them the power of distributing the nation's wealth— two for me, one for you. Such selfish motives lead over-ambitious characters to support even ideas that have always failed--if they can be used to fool the voters.

4. Many people, unaware of the simple lessons of history, or able to ignore those realities for feel-good notions, can become virtual missionaries for even unattainable ideas.

5. Our educators have not taught any understanding of socialism and present it as a way to help the poor and disadvantaged. But the safety-nets that provide welfare for the needy

are accepted by virtually everyone; they are alive and well in every capitalist nation. Welfare has nothing to do with socialism.

6. Both socialism and communism involve the takeover of a nation's businesses by politicians. That is unworkable because governmental bureaucracies are rarely managed as well as private companies. (Imagine the results if Bernie Sanders or Nancy Pelosi had the power to dictate management decisions to the presidents of Johnson & Johnson, Apple, Procter & Gamble, Home Depot, Microsoft, or Costco Markets!)

7. Finally, the reality: The true choice is not between "public corruption or private plunder." There are two forms of capitalism: One that is well regulated and one that is excessively regulated. The latter, whether called mercantilism, socialism, or communism, is inefficient and often corrupted by the government bureaucracy.

8. True capitalism, if regulated with only one end in mind—maintaining a just and open economy operating under rules to minimize cheating—is not "private plunder." The "plunder" only happens when elites twist the rules to their own advantage!

The best choice is clear: Public corruption can never be totally eliminated because we will never find enough Saints to fill the offices of government. The only way to keep government officials honest is to limit their power. Socialism in all its forms gives government officials *more* power.

The realistic solution is to maintain true capitalism by simply enforcing the rules needed to keep the business sphere open to all on an equal basis. The only way to keep capitalism fair and minimize unfair tactics by the greedy is to keep the elites from manipulating the rules.

It all comes back to the need for the public to control the elites. That can be done if voters get informed and stay vigilant. It is the only way to maintain a prosperous economy with equal opportunity for all. Otherwise, lazy voters will get the government they deserve—a bad one!

Townhall's Marina Medvin recently wrote an essay comparing Bernie Sanders' appeal "to that of a man in a van luring unsuspecting kids inside with promises of candy and puppies.... Today's youngest voters grew up tightly packed in bubble wrap...never getting to understand reality.... If you grow up with white-glove care from a nanny, why wouldn't you ask for a nanny-state to continue coddling you through your illusory adulthood? (And illusory it often is.)"

Ms. Medved thus points out that Autocrats promote socialism because it lulls the public into accepting "candy" from the government and makes them easier to rule over:

> "I received a historically accurate education about the evils of socialism and the forced division of wealth, and I can navigate through a politician's fairy tales. It's not as easy for a generation bubble-wrapped to see past the puppies.... Young voters did not grow up understanding the consequences of what Bernie proposes or what Stalin, Che, and Mao did to their people. They don't ask questions about what happens when the working class isn't motivated to keep working and just shrugs.

> "Bernie has simply taken advantage of what public education has served him on a silver platter: Marxist youths. Duping young adults lacking historical perspective is all too easy with unattainable promises. That is how socialism has risen from the dead."[110]

However, the real choice is not private plunder or public corruption. Each citizen must choose whether he or she will take some time to follow the political scene and support only honest candidates dedicated to fair and efficient government or just go with the party that claims to satisfy his material interests. In short, forget the candy and puppies; look for experience, integrity, and proven competency.

WHY DON'T THE SCHOOLS TEACH USEFUL KNOWLEDGE?

It is no coincidence that the "bubble wrapped" people Medved described were educated in our government-run schools, where the curriculum advocates the role of a big "nanny" government, and the textbooks all toe the line required by current PC standards. The Durants' excellent history books and many others that do not present the currently accepted ideological view are excluded from their courses. Instead, the students get a one-sided and distorted education designed to shape their political thinking, a blatant censorship that has never helped the common people.

GOVERNMENT-RUN SCHOOLS

"He who owns the youth, owns the future

ADOLPH HITLER

"Give me just one generation of youth and I'll transform the whole world."

VLADIMIR LENIN

Education is supposed to encourage rational thinking and debate, not the mindless acceptance of political indoctrination. Mark Bauerlein has called attention to this issue, and it contains a stark message for those who continue to debate irrelevant theories: "For 30 years, conservatives have won many debates, issued best-selling books, and swayed public opinion in many areas, but they haven't slowed the long march of the radicals through the institutions at all. For example, Allan Bloom's *The Closing of the American Mind* and writings by Roger Kimball, Dinesh D'Souza, Richard Bernstein, and countless others convinced the public that political correctness was becoming a serious problem on college campuses, but the coercive uniformity of opinion in higher education has only gotten worse since then. While the Right was beating them in the ideas arena, the Left was claiming office space."[111]

Bauerlein correctly points out that most voters do not give a whit about complicated economic or political theory. The conservative writers are read by a very small group and are literally "preaching to the choir." Meanwhile, the educational establishment is instilling a combination of ignorance and bias in their students' heads. Graduates end up believing that unlimited distributions from government are available and there are no limits on amounts because billionaires and corporations have so much! Personal freedom and national bankruptcy are never mentioned.

A school system that finances an extension of adolescence for youth 17-22 years old, while saddling them with heavy debt, is not the way to prepare "the future builders of America" for responsible adulthood. In fact, it is deliberately designed to create an ideologically conformed class of political and economic ignoramuses with a permanent dependency on maternal protection. Today's schools produce creatures quite different from the working families' youth of yesterday who were sent to work or apprenticed at an early age, aware of the need to make their own way in life. Why must we tolerate that emasculation of our children?

THE SECRET PLANS TO CONTROL THE MINDS OF OUR PEOPLE

The elites game plan has for centuries concentrated on controlling the ideas implanted in the student's brains so that they are more pliable subjects, ignorant of politics and finance, and more easily forced to comply with their leaders demands. The worst autocrats in Nazi Germany and Communist Russia made such intentions perfectly clear. They believed that by the indoctrination of the youth they could create a permanent class of docile subjects.

Sadly, that dumbing down conspiracy has not been confined to dictatorships but is happening right here in America. Mark Mullen has pointed out that only 35% of our fourth graders are proficient in writing, that consequently the remaining 65% will never be proficient, and that the educational elites planned for that result. And Congress helped them. "Together, they don't want smart kids. Actually, they don't want smart adults."[112]

Candace Owens has reported that our billionaires are using their vast wealth and their tax-exempt foundations to help make our kids stupid: "Bill Gates is spending $1.7 Billion to "help" with what he views to be problematic: math. Gates says math suffers from — you guessed it — white supremacy, so he's put forth an equitable math curriculum. His organization, Equitablemath.org, describes the problem with math being the white supremacist notion that in order to be "right," students must get the correct answer in class. Now, in order to foster "equity," they want to make *every* answer correct in classrooms across the country. To put it another way, they're going to make your kids stupid in the name of fighting white supremacy and furthering equity."

Almost 100 years ago, radical professors headed the Progressive Education movement. Mark Mullen relates how a teacher by the name of Nelson was invited to join a meeting of thirteen leading educators and later reported that "all thirteen were paid members of the Communist Party of Russia… The sole work of the group was to destroy our schools!"[113] During the meeting Nelson questioned the adoption of "modern math" because he pointed out it relied on memorization rather than reasoning. A Dr. Ziegler replied, "Nelson, wake up! That is what we want… a math that the pupils cannot apply to life situations when they get out of school."

Mullen devotes over twenty pages to listing the proposals from leading members of the National Education Association to manipulate the public-school curricula. The cited proposals come from every decade since 1920! That is how persistent those educational experts have been to subvert the country's population. The recommended tweaks to our school curricula came from professors of Education at many of the nation's leading universities. In 1968, one of them suggested that "the first educational question will not be what knowledge is of the most worth? But what kinds of human beings do we wish to produce?"

In 1973, at a gathering in Denver, Harvard professor Chester M. Pierce stated, "Every child in America entering school at the age of five is insane… with allegiances toward our Founding Fathers, towards his parents… toward a belief in a supernatural being, and toward the sovereignty of this nation as a separate entity. It's up to you, teachers, to make all these sick children well by creating the international child of the future."[114]

As recently as 2016, First Lady Michelle Obama declared "the choice in this election is about who will have the power to shape our children for the next four years of their lives."[115] As it turned out, Donald Trump won the election and appointed a strong advocate of Charter Schools to head the DEA, a blessing for school choice, but one being reversed in 2021 following President Biden's election.

It is frightening to discover that the century-long debate over the curricula used in our schools has not been a legitimate intellectual exploration of what is best for the children and our country. Most Americans have believed that claims about a diabolical plot to transform American children was just another "conspiracy theory." But the mystery has been solved—there is in truth an inner circle of people desiring to advance their ideological goals by "shaping" our children into passionate followers of the elites' directives. And many of those people appear to be active in our highest educational institutions. Recent moves to exclude parents from having any say over their school's curricula shows that the battle by elites to control our children is gaining momentum.

WOODROW WILSON, EDWARD BERNAYS, AND THE MANIPULATION OF THE MASSES

The effort by American elites to control how their citizens think and behave received a big boost in the early 1900s when President Woodrow Wilson signed an executive order establishing a new federal agency, the Committee on Public Information, often dubbed as a "Ministry of Information." The CPI was in effect a major effort in propaganda, designed to shape the thinking of Americans into supporting our entry into the European war.

WHAT ELITES WANT

They want more for themselves and less for everybody else... That's why education will never ever get better... They don't want a population of citizens capable of critical thinking... That doesn't help them.... They want OBEDIENT WORKERS. People who are just smart enough to run the machines and do the paperwork and just dumb enough to passively accept all these increasingly shittier jobs with the lower pay, the longer hours, the reduced benefits.

GEORGE CARLIN – *THE AMERICAN DREAM*

One important employee at the CPI was Edward Bernays (1891-1995), a nephew of Sigmund Freud, and his contribution centered on a new scientific basis for manipulating public opinion. In his book, *Propaganda*, Bernays explained that "The conscious and intelligent manipulation of the organized habits and opinions of the masses is an important element in democratic society.... Those who manipulate this unseen mechanism of society constitute an invisible government which is the true ruling power of our country."[116]

Using methods that he called the "engineering of consent," Bernays helped promote the war to the American people as one that would "Make the World Safe for Democracy." Those techniques have provided a model to market subsequent wars. However, after the war, Bernays warned us that: "We are governed, our minds are molded, our tastes formed, our ideas suggested, largely by men who we have never heard of."

By such tactics, as well as by currying the support of the media, and influencing what is taught in the schools, our elites have for the last century been manipulating the public's ideas and opinions. No wonder we over-extend our credit cards and re-elect known crooks!

This author must admit that he was exceedingly slow to accept the reality that government agencies are actively shaping the voters' opinions by psychological methods. We can understand that politicians will promise good things, and we take that for what it's worth, but to be subjected to subliminal and manipulative propaganda seems beyond the pale. It comes as an equal surprise to realize that our supposedly dedicated educational experts are not working to improve the quality of instruction but to lower it—and to slant it to further their political goals!

WHY NOT REPLACE DIVISIVE INDOCTRINATION WITH USEFUL SKILLS AND ESSENTIAL KNOWLEDGE

In recent years, the movement to enforce politically correct speech and cancel our traditional culture, is evidence of how far the elites are determined to go to gain control over the minds of our country's citizens. The truth seems to be that both the schools and the government do everything to deceive us! How can that be? Withholding useful knowledge and inserting destructive ideas into our minds is treasonous. It's deliberate sabotage, like polluting our water supply or fanning the flames of prejudice, hate, and division. But it does seem quite arguable that there is more than paranoia or an affinity for conspiracy theories involved.

Americans are products of their culture—somewhat naïve, cooperative, and trusting. Our ways of thinking were ingrained in our cultural roots and our ideas of sportsmanship. It is difficult for most people to believe that leading professionals in government and education are pursuing personal radical theories with the intent to graduate unquestioning obedient workers to the workforce. But that is what they are doing. The Common Core Curriculum, and the fine-sounding No-Child-Left-Behind program, are designed to shape the thinking of our children. In 2010, the National Governors Association and the Chief State School Officers, brought forth The Common Core State Standards as the curriculum for all U. S. public schools. That program was supported by the U. S. Department of Education, the American Federation of Teachers, the National Education Association, and was funded by the Bill and Melinda Gates Foundation, and 46 states adopted the standards. More recently, "Critical Race Theory" has been introduced to denigrate American culture and create more "victims," and thereby tighten the elite's control.

It is noteworthy that those standards and policies reflect the *Education for All* program introduced by UNESCO in 2000 which directs school curriculum toward a globalist and communal/socialist agenda. Mark Mullen describes these policies as a blatant attempt to create a New World Order as outlined in UNESCO's *"Education 2030: A Framework for Action."* That monograph proposes that the United Nations create a curriculum for all nations. One of the standards proposed has been adopted by 46 American states and illustrates their goal: the English Language Arts standard requires that 50% of reading instructions be informational and nonfiction text. Mark Mullen has pointed out that "the informational articles" are chosen for their advocacy of certain political and social policies: "The standards are just an extension of UNESCO's drive to gain control of the world's children, who will grow into obedient global adults with attachment to no country to call home."[117]

WHY SO MANY TESTS?

"Common Core supporters tell us they are NOT writing the curricula, only the tests. But when you control the tests, you control the curriculum."

(CONCERNED WOMEN FOR AMERICA, CCNCPRESENTATION.PDF)

The standards are designed to have the students memorize and parrot back what they have been taught, with little emphasis on independent thought of their own. Mullen quotes Alex Newman's opinion that these standards "were designed to teach students what to think and not how to think. The literary classics have been stripped and replaced with books promoting a socialist agenda."[118]

The new standards also require significant time spent on testing which has proven so stressful to students that many parents opt out of giving the tests to their children. However, pressure has been applied by the U. S. government to enforce the taking of every test the bureaucrats have prescribed: The federal government requires that every state submit a detailed accountability plan addressing how the state will force parents to allow the testing. And the big stick is that, if such a plan is not submitted, the state could lose its federal funding.[119] Thus, the long-standing tradition of local control over our schools will be quickly usurped by the federal government. If ever there was a reason to eliminate the Department of Education, we can see it here.

Note that in the presidential debates of 15-20 years ago, candidates openly advocated the elimination of several government agencies, a reform still attractive to many. We already have competent educators, Superintendents, and school boards in every community to oversee our schools. What can a vast agency in Washington be needed for other than to impose undesirable rules for those schools to adhere to?

Now, most classroom teachers are a dedicated group intent on helping their students. But their materials and curricula are dictated by a remote establishment run by individuals advancing an anti-democratic ideology. Today's schools and colleges are turning back the clock to the closed thinking and conforming mindsets, the servile peasant mentality established in the past by autocratic despots. They are well on the way to recreating a submissive mentality in our citizenry. The students would be better served by learning more about investments, personal finance, home mortgages, credit cards, debt amortization, inflation, and compound interest than being forced to spend time being tested to make sure that they can regurgitate the desired "instructional material."

SUMMARY

Throughout history despots have tried in every way to control their people. In recent centuries, these efforts have moved from sheer physical oppression to more subtle forms of psychological conditioning. The horrors inflicted by 20th century rulers in Nazi Germany and Communist China and Russia gained support from their people by using state-run schools and a controlled media to condition their people. It is very apparent that those same techniques are much in use today in Western democracies where "progressive" puppeteers are busily shaping the minds and attitudes of our youth.

A related process employed by elites is to pose as economic experts managing the economy. Academics have helped this ruse by promoting economic courses that explain how effectively the economy can be managed. Of course, the elite's real goal is to manipulate the economy, so it helps themselves. Indeed, they have made the study of monetary policy so complicated that no citizen can make sense of what they are saying. As one academic observer wrote, "In the wake of the catastrophic events of September 11, 2001… Macro-economics 2001 came equipped with a new and bewildering set of concepts that include slinky terms like … information cascades, adaptive behavior, market friction, diffusion rates, and other such exotica."[120]

To bolster their importance, the economists have proven expert at delivering impressive sounding jargon such as: "The stagflation of the 1970s required a thorough conceptual overhaul of economic thinking and policymaking. Monetarism, and new insights into the effects of anticipatory expectations on economic activity and price setting, competed strongly against the traditional Keynesianism."[121] Clearly, the study of economics has changed considerably since its origins, but the clarity of its practitioners has seriously declined.

In the next chapter, we learn about the earliest economists, from the seventeenth century, who were not yet buried in abstruse conceptualizations. They described how the beneficial power of free market capitalism was being clearly illustrated by the entrepreneurs involved in Europe's surging agricultural activity. Unfortunately, as economists gained influence, they have added a lot of academic gobble-de-gook to their theorizing.

CHAPTER 10-

The Rise of Economics: A Soft Science

Governments live off their citizens so…they are inevitably parasites. By taking over functions which used to be a matter for society, however, they become something more like a malignant tumor
Ivo Mosley: In the Name of the People, 123

Homo sapiens have engaged in *economic activity* ever since the first cave man exchanged some sharpened flint stones for fresh caught fish or a few bananas. Since then, the only major change in such business activity has been the use of money as a medium of exchange, banks to hold and lend money, and the degree of regulation imposed by governments. Economists arrived only recently and are still trying to make sense of the business activities that people have been engaged in for the last few tens of thousands of years. And, because they are not true scientists, they have made a real muddle out of what is little more than exchanging one thing for another.

Adam Smith's *Wealth of Nations* is often cited as the beginning of *economics* as an academic subject but 100 years before Adam Smith, William Petty was developing an explanation

"…based on a series of practical examples to illustrate how things worked. In other words, he was describing an already existing capitalist economy… Many of his examples were drawn from Holland's sophisticated banking and stock exchange structure that enabled it to finance a gigantic trade with the Far East."[122]

The son of a village tailor, Petty paid for his education and an apprenticeship as a mariner by gambling and writing letters for the illiterate. Petty's ideas about "economics," put forward in three essays published in the 1660s, were based on how a revolutionary extension of free economic opportunity to many individuals had emerged from a revolution in land ownership: That recent expansion in the number of economic participants had marked "the precise point at which capitalism and private property can be seen to have merged."[123]

King Henry VIII confiscated the Church's farmland and then sold it to his subjects to pay for his foreign wars.

Ironically, we owe the notorious King Henry VIII some credit for that revolution in land ownership. In 1517 Martin Luther had opened a Pandora's Box by challenging the authority of the Catholic Church. Then, in 1531, the king, empowered by the Protestant Revolution, declared himself head of the church of England. His goal (besides wanting a quick divorce) was to confiscate the holdings of the Catholic monasteries that had acquired over two million acres of land, or about 20 percent of the cultivated farmland in England.[124] By 1550 that land was in the king's hands and he sold much of it to pay for his foreign wars—a perfect example of what elites do; take money from their people so they can engage in foreign wars!

REDISCOVERING THE POWER OF PRIVATE PROPERTY

That vast acreage was subsequently divided into smaller parcels and resold so that "within two generations...its eventual destination was not the ancient nobility, but people with cash--London merchants, careful farmers, government officials, even tenants on fixed rents--anyone looking for a secure investment."[125] That may have been one of history's most significant distributions of land that benefitted the common people—it allowed many individuals to become owners of their homes as well as secure participants in their country's economy.

By 1580, this opening up of the land began to pay a dividend: the new owners had sought every possible way to make their land more profitable. As a result, agricultural productivity had soared. The spirit of free enterprise and the reward of increased wealth had changed the economy.

At the same time, England's population doubled in one century, reaching four million in 1600. But, instead of food shortages, the increased yields from the farms resulted in declining prices for food and an improvement in the general diet. Milk, butter, cheese, and meat became more plentiful and less expensive. "For the first time in European history, a society was about to escape the choke on population growth that was created by subsistence farming."[126] That revolution in land ownership also exposed the difference between what had become two competing forms of capitalism—the true *free* form and a *corrupt* form manipulated by elites for their own advantage.

Europe's leaders had to that point only allowed a slightly open economy known as mercantilism: The king granted monopolies in each trade and the businesses remained heavily regulated and taxed by the governments. Those large monopolies brought in immense profits from trade with the new lands recently discovered all around the world, but that overly regulated form of capitalism did not possess the full power of "true" capitalism. Under mercantilism, there is less choice and higher prices. Fortunately, that semi-feudal system was gradually broken at the rural farm level by opening-up a free market in land for ordinary people.

The problem I have with the Trusts... is the fact that they were the greatest enemies of capitalism. Without a free market you cannot have freedom itself.

JIM RUMFORD, TOBACCO, TRUSTS & TRUMP

The workings of true capitalism, as exemplified by the many new owners of agricultural land, provided William Petty with the perfect case study of free enterprise in action. Unfortunately, Petty's "discovery" of free markets lay dormant because the elites wanted mercantilism to dominate industrial trade. However, a hundred years later, in the mid-1700s, Petty's observations found a home with the physiocrats in Paris who supported the belief that free markets and true capitalism were preferable to the regulated form under mercantilism. It was at that time, in 1763, that Adam Smith arrived in Paris to visit Dr. Francois de Quesnay, an originating champion of the Laissez-Faire ideas that advocated free and open economies.

One of de Quesnay's associates was the Irish-born, Paris-based Richard Cantillon, who had published his famous essay on free markets in 1732. As Andro Linklater writes, Cantillon's "first two sentences were lifted straight from William Petty: 'Land is the source (of) all wealth. Human labor is the form which produces it.' In other words, the physiocrats' economic model was based on conditions in seventeenth-century England."[127]

Adam Smith remained in Paris with these free market economists for two years, gaining the foundational material for *The Wealth of Nations* which was published in 1776. There he criticized mercantilism as an overly regulated and top-down management of capitalism and set forth the advantages of a free and competitive market. It is a testament to the persistence of elites that 100 years later, the bankers and robber barons in America still had to be prosecuted to minimize their unfair and monopolistic business practices.[128]

Adam Smith gets the credit for the initial observations of Petty and the French physiocrats, but another unsung hero was Anders Chydenius, a Swedish pastor and teacher, who anticipated Adam Smith's work by eleven years, publishing *The National Gain* in 1765. In an essay about Chydenius' role, Professor Gary Galles recently wrote:

"I especially resonated with Carl Uhr's description of Chydenius as 'imbued... by the vision that man, in seeking his own gain by specialization of labor and by exchange under an impersonal discipline of competition, would realize ... the welfare and progress of society as a whole.' I only wish that, a quarter millennia later, more people shared Chydenius's insight that, in Eli Heckscher's words, 'the only path to social harmony ... was by free competition ... all governmental intervention in the production and distribution of goods and services redounded sooner or later to the disadvantage of the great majority of the people.'"[129]

Thus, the value of free markets, and the evils of managed mercantilist economies, was widely recognized in the 18th century by many people. Chydenius was a self-educated pastor who wrote his books in Swedish but had come to the same conclusions as Adam Smith simply by observing the actual operation of his country's business activities.

Further evidence confirming the value of a free market was the vibrant business activities in colonial America. More than a century before Adam Smith set pen to paper, settlers in the American colonies were enjoying their economic freedom to build thriving farming, fishing, and trading businesses within a purely capitalistic economy. Even Petty, in the 1660s, could have observed free enterprise already in action in the American colonies. Indeed, by the time Adam Smith returned from Paris to England the American revolution was close at hand because the elites in England had attempted to limit the colonists' liberty—they wanted to impose a stamp tax and dictate restrictions on navigation. Fortunately, the freedom loving Liberty Boys would not tolerate even those small limits on their business activities. They had a "zero tolerance" for restrictions coming from the top!

During the next 150 years, the newly independent Americans conducted business under a form of pure capitalism and established their worldwide economic and industrial supremacy. Their success was assisted by the fact that the European nations were slow to abandon the harmful drag of their mercantile economies. Another case of winning by the default of others. It is indicative of how simple the study of *economics* can be that these practical observers of the world around them were able so easily to note the fundamental principles governing how nations gain success.

WHY DO SO MANY OPPOSE THE FREE MARKET?

Currently, in America, after more than 350 years of its demonstrated effectiveness, the nature of free markets remains a contested subject. The academics, economists, and media pundits who shape our national policies, have been extraordinarily successful in claiming themselves to be the real architects of progress and blocking any suggestion that material advances come from the work of many ordinary individuals.

Their "success" in that ruse is evidenced by how the elites have gradually twisted the American economy into what we now know as "crony capitalism," which is nothing more than a modern equivalent of mercantilism. It is a clear case of what Yogi Berra called "*deja-vu* all over again." After centuries of a great people building a new nation's freedom and growth, the elites have wormed their way into power. They are called "progressives," but they are the ones that want to turn back the clock to sixteenth century feudal oppression.

It is clear evidence of the harmful influence of elites that we are still debating basic economic principles that were clearly enunciated 350 years ago by William Petty. This is not a complicated subject: The basic principle is simply that having many participants in an open economy will create more innovation, more prosperity, for more people, than can be achieved by a managed economy regulated by "experts" at the top. The elites are working overtime to bury that truth.

Anyone who wants to help elites maintain their superior positions has had to join that conspiracy and claim that it is the elites who produce prosperity—not the many imaginative and highly motivated, engineers, physical scientists, merchants, janitors, laborers, farmers, and even the bankers and lawyers. Because their argument is so patently ridiculous, the "experts" have tried to convince voters that "economics" is a complex theoretical pursuit.

Unfortunately, by subjecting economics to complex abstractions, they have allowed all sorts of theorists to develop all sorts of theories. That is why "economics" has abandoned the real world of business transactions, created a bewildering set of polysyllabic jargon, and is riven by disagreement among its professionals, who, it has been said, even when laid end to end, never reach a conclusion. For example, in 1798, another famous economist, who rejected all that Petty and Smith had concluded, published a doomsday scenario predicting that exponential increases in population growth would surpass the meager arithmetical increases in food supply.

Mass starvation would result he wrote unless population growth was arrested by government actions. Thomas Malthus apparently overlooked the rapid increase in the human population that had been going on, as was explained in chapter one, for the prior 70,000 years! He also set aside the detailed studies of Adam Smith and ignored the fact that the English population had doubled from two to four million during the 16th century yet gained a better diet and an increased supply of food.

Malthusian ideas have been largely discredited over the last two centuries by a continuing increase in productivity, but they still remain popular. Malthusian logic is flawed, but because it supports the idea that we need managers at the top layers of government to control populations and production, it is often promoted by the elites who relish such top-down jobs and the opportunity to speculate ad infinitum on what to do next.

Then, as if Malthus had not done enough harm, Karl Marx came out of the woodwork in 1867, and outlined the superiority of communal economies that would be totally controlled by an elite leadership group.[130] He correctly criticized capitalism for its monopolies and labor strife, which were somewhat reformed in America a few decades later by anti-trust laws and court rulings. However, his ideas on abolishing private property and forcing workers to toil in communal farms were based on utopian fantasies, and have been proven to be both inefficient, barbaric, and authoritarian in the extreme.

The biggest failing of those advocating radical change is to not recognize the actual results of different economic systems. Corrupt as the Western democratic nations are, and even with the tilted rules that aid the wealthy, the bottom fifth of American families enjoy a higher disposable income than the average citizen of every other nation on earth. Think how much better that could be if the unfair stratagems of the elites were removed from the American economy. Then, the families of our lowest fifth might exceed everyone else's top fifth!

In the 1920s and 1930s the Russian dictator, Josef Stalin, demonstrated the folly of Marxian communism by his gruesome efforts to enforce the collectivization of Russian farms. Although, that program resulted in the starvation or imprisonment of more than 10 million of his citizens, and failed to promote prosperity, there still are many advocates passionately devoted to the dream of universal equality and its "the end justifies the means" methodology.

WHY LIBERALS LOVE BIG GOVERNMENT

"INSIDE EVERY PROGRESSIVE IS A TOTALITARIAN SCREAMING TO GET OUT"

@HOROWITZ39, DAVID HOROWITZ

Take a moment to think that over: The Russian communist leaders had a theoretical dream to create a better society and to get there they were willing to kill over 10 million of their people. It failed, but then Pol

Pot tried the same thing in Cambodia. And Chairman Mao did the same thing in China. All three of those national atrocities were imposed by an elite who gained control of the authoritarian reins of their governments.[131] Each of those successive "experiments" in the laboratory of history killed millions of people and proved to be failures. Statistically speaking, the trial runs were one hundred percent failures.

HISTORICAL EXPERIENCE TRUMPS ABSTRACT THINKING

For all its warts, the free market and its respect for the life and liberty of every citizen has been proven the better model for a nation's people. Those nations that maintained a relatively free market have consistently enjoyed higher standards of living and more disposable income than those living in controlled economies. Yet many academics, intellectuals, and economic theorists keep proposing "modifications" because they want jobs manipulating the economy. It is worth noting that very few of their proposed modifications address the corruption of the elites who distort the marketplace for their own benefit.

We must recognize that the current controversy about what causes the rise of successful nations does not represent a legitimate intellectual debate; it is a veritable war with the elites wanting to gain the power to tilt the rules to their advantage and the people wanting a free and just marketplace. That is why 350 years after Petty, and more than 200 years after Smith, in 1981, the advantage of a truly free market still had to be demonstrated by Julian Simon:

> "It is a simple fact that the source of improvements in productivity is the human mind, and a human mind is seldom found apart from a human body. And because improvements—their invention and their adoption—come from people, it seems reasonable to assume that the amount of improvement depends on the number of people available to use their minds. This is an old idea, going back at least as far as William Petty in 1682."[132]

Despite what Simon wrote, however, the dispute continues. The elites have to keep the debate alive. To do otherwise would be an admission that all their critiques, suggestions, and analyses were of little value; that the people could do it all without their interference!

HOW CAPITALISM SHED THE BURDEN OF MERCANTILIST REGULATION

The fundamental weakness of the mercantile economic system was that the government licensed only a few manufacturers in each industry. This made tax collection easier but prevented the great efficiency and wide choice available in a free economy open to all entrepreneurs. Just as Prohibition in America in the 1930s created an underground economy for liquor, the many legal restrictions of Mercantilism created a demand for a wider, but illegal, availability of commodities.

Two great historians have described how the free market itself gradually eliminated the mercantilist overly regulated economies of Europe:

> "There was no sudden repeal of price controls… Rather, in a development traceable from small beginnings in twelfth-century Northern Italy, enterprising merchants and artisans searched out more and more opportunities for relatively unregulated trade and manufacture until, by the end of the eighteenth century, the older forms of trade by 'regulated companies'…had become moribund."[133]

Professors Rosenberg and Birdzell almost credit ordinary people for this remarkable transformation to free capitalistic economies:

> "Aggressive individuals could and did evade guild authority by establishing enterprises in the countryside…. As merchants succeeded more and more in

escaping political control, they ventured into trade in more commodities and between more places.... This trade, and its profits, helped produce a merchant class who lived by buying and selling.... The West's sustained economic growth began with the emergence of an economic sphere with a higher degree of autonomy from political and religious control."[134]

These two authors almost confirm that economic progress came, not from ideas or theories, but from the actual work-a-day activities of people:

"The dominant fact...(was) their wholly pragmatic character and their lack of ideological commitment to any economic principle other than their economic effectiveness and survivability. The system that generated Western economic growth evolved before it was recognized as a system or advocated as an ideology."[135]

In that way, those authors confirm that theories and ideas were not involved in economic progress. And, in their conclusion, after referring to all the usual geographic factors they do suggest:

"The West's achievement of autonomy stemmed from a relaxation, or a weakening, of political and religious controls, giving other departments of social life the opportunity to experiment with change.... A *successful* change requires a large measure of freedom to experiment (and) costs a society's rulers their feeling of control, as if they were conceding to others the power to determine the society's future. The great majority of societies, past and present, have not allowed it. Nor have they escaped poverty."[136]

Thus, without actually saying it, these two authors are agreeing with the theme of this book that it was the freedom to act, "the weakening of controls," that allowed ordinary working folks to create economic progress and prosperity and that in most of the world, it was "their rulers" who prevented them from so acting. Such books, that once provided a window to the truth, have been replaced in our schoolrooms by newer pro-big-government texts that meet the approval of today's ruling class.

SUMMARY

The historical record, that free competition beat state-run economies, gradually led to a fuller blossoming of a free market in England as well as the decline of mercantilist systems. It is worth noting that the same lesson had been already established by the flood of settlers that had left England and initiated scores of small independent farms and businesses in the English colonies around the world. And those economies succeeded with little or no government, and long before the Enlightenment scholars wrote about it--another example of how ordinary workers and businesspeople had to build the modern economy before the experts could tell them how to do it!

There is a connection between political freedom and economic freedom. The people of Europe understood the need for both and their 1000-year struggle to gain such freedom was won very gradually because the elites resisted any type of liberalization. However, during the last four centuries the people have made progress on both fronts. Unfortunately, free people are never safe from elites. The elites never sleep. And in most free nations their tactic has been to corrupt the free market that they despise. How they do that, and how we can limit the damage they do, is the subject of the following chapter.

CHAPTER 11-

Why Free Markets Must Have Honest Referees

"The problem you run into…is that the same bigotry and prejudice and lust for power that can infect a capitalist system can infect any other system as well.

"This is about the need for vigilance in our rules, why we need rules that are fair and that are consistently enforced. If we do that, markets will produce great value and great opportunity for our people. And if we don't have those rules, replacing the market part of the system is not going to help."[137]

Senator Elizabeth Warren

T HE DEVIOUS METHODS THAT ELITES use to tilt the rules to their own advantage was meticulously detailed in G. Edward Griffin's book "The Creature from Jekyll Island," Within its massive 608 pages the author tells an interesting story: How America's most powerful financial tycoons arranged for President Wilson to sign into law the Federal Reserve System, a quasi-governmental organization that would determine the future of our banking and monetary policy. The message put out was that the Federal Reserve would help maintain an orderly economy and thereby help all the people of America. Few people recognized that such an agency, supposedly a watchdog for the people, might not always serve as an honest referee.

Griffin knows how to make complex sleep-inducing material come alive. He opens his book by describing a secret meeting of six powerful bankers in a New Jersey train station:

"The railway station was bitterly cold that night... November winds rattled roof panels above the track... It was approaching ten P. M., and the station was nearly empty... For those with limited funds, coach cars were coupled to the front...the environment was drab.

"In their hurry to board the train and escape the chill of the wind, few passengers noticed the activity at the far end of the platform. At a gate seldom used at this hour of the night was a spectacular sight... a long car that caused those few who saw it to stop and stare. Its gleaming black paint was accented with polished brass handrails... The shades were drawn, but through the open door, one could see mahogany paneling, velvet drapes, plush armchairs, and a well-stocked bar... On the center of each side was a small plaque bearing but a single word: ALDRICH.

"The name of Nelson Aldrich, senator from Rhode Island, was well known even in New Jersey... his private railway car was often seen...during frequent trips to Wall Street... His son-in-law was John D. Rockefeller, Jr. Sixty years later his grandson, Nelson Aldrich Rockefeller, would become Vice-President of the United States."[138]

Griffin continues to explain how five men appeared at that railway station separately and joined Senator Aldrich in his opulent car. In addition to Aldrich, they were the Assistant Secretary of the U.S. Treasury, the president of the most powerful bank of the time, a senior partner at J.P. Morgan Company, the head of the J.P. Morgan' Bankers Trust Company, and a representative of the banking dynasty in England and France whose brother was head of the Warburg banking consortium in Germany and the Netherlands. The six men "represented an estimated one-fourth of the total wealth of the entire world."[139]

The private railway car ended its journey in a small fishing village in Brunswick, Georgia. Locals were told that the group were avid duck hunters going to stay at the lodge on Jekyll Island recently bought by J.P. Morgan and some associates. However, Griffin explains their purpose differently:

"Simply stated, the purpose was to come to an agreement on the structure and operation of a banking cartel. The goal, as is true with all cartels, was to maximize profits by minimizing competition between members, to make it difficult for new competitors to enter the field, and to utilize the police powers of the government to enforce the cartel agreement. In more specific terms, it was to create a blueprint for the Federal Reserve System."[140]

The immediate stimulus to their meeting had been the recent proliferation of banks throughout the country that was eroding the dominance of New York banks. "In 1910, the number of banks in the United States…had more than doubled to over ten thousand in just the previous ten years… Most…were in the South and West, causing the New York banks to suffer a steady decline in market share… By 1913, when the Federal Reserve Act was passed those…non-national banks (held) fifty-seven percent of the deposits. In the eyes of those 'duck hunters' from New York, this was a trend that simply had to be reversed."[141]

BECAUSE PEOPLE ARE OUR PRIME ASSET, REGULATIONS MUST PROVIDE THEM EQUAL OPPORTUNITY

Griffin's allegations have been dismissed as a mere conspiracy theory by many establishment figures. However, in 1987, William

Greider published *Secrets of the Temple* that also provides details about those six men and the workings of the Federal Reserve that they helped create. Greider details the Reserve's strengths and weaknesses without excess criticism, but comments how after 74 years, the financiers involved still needed to "fine-tune" their management of the economy. And Greider does give his readers a conclusion similar to Griffin's when he tells us that many well-meaning reformers supported the bankers' plan because they hoped that "a government system would finally harness the 'money trust,' disarm its powers, and establish broad democratic control over money and credit (this version became the historian's standard interpretation). ... The results were nearly the opposite... Once the Fed was in operation, the steady diffusion of financial power halted. Wall Street maintained its dominant position— and even enhanced it—until the trauma of 1929."[142]

This dismal story of the Fed's origins is just one example of how, over, and over, throughout history, the elites have sold the public complicated approaches to "make things better" for the people. Both Griffin and Greider detail how the advocates of the Federal Reserve carefully crafted their proposals as ones that would help the people and the nation. And they both agree that such "reforms" actually worked in reverse—because the fine print had been designed to help the elites and make the people pay for it all. This deception, to advocate something as helpful to the people, even though it is actually harmful, is still in use today: President Biden's multi-trillion dollar "Infrastructure Bill" allocates 80% of that figure to non-infrastructure projects and only 20% to infrastructure.

It is ironic that many well-intentioned reformers are drawn to proposals that give outsized power to the government to solve problems. In the case of the Federal Reserve, well-meaning reformers bit, hook, line, and sinker, for the bankers' argument that the Federal Reserve would make the financial sector more responsive to the people. Similarly, most Americans supported President Bush's Iraq War because we were told that it would protect America's "vital interests" in the Middle East! Kind-hearted people supported President Johnson's "War on Poverty" that decimated America's families and created a flood of single parent homes. Greedy elites love those kinds of gullible people. They will always encourage any reformers who seek to grant more power to the government. The more power the federal government gets, the more wealth the elites can divert to themselves.

Teddy Roosevelt spoke softly but carried a big stick to whack the monopolies!

Around the beginning of the twentieth century, the legendary "Trust Busters" Teddy Roosevelt and Howard Taft had sought to restore fair competition in America's marketplace. Many giant monopolies were broken up, trade unions were supported with enabling laws, all to battle the growing power of huge corporations that dominated the economy. Then, during Woodrow Wilson's eight-year presidency, from 1912 to 1920, the pendulum swung away from such needed reforms and in favor of the powerful, giving the six bankers from Jekyll Island what they wanted: The Federal Reserve System.

After that, the American government grew, its youth were sent to fight foreign wars, and income taxes were imposed to pay for it all. The English Kings of yore would cheer all those developments—they loved their lavish courts, wars, and taxes on the people!

The endless foreign wars and the violence and partisan bitterness that has muddied many countries in recent years confirm that, like those six bankers that met on Jekyll Island, most leaders are not concerned with we the people but primarily pursue their own obscene fortunes. In fact, they show little regard for the masses of ordinary citizens who make the factories hum and our families prosper.

The majority of our elite leaders have now joined forces with the academics, the media, the experts, and the pundits to transform America. Most ordinary people have been excluded, taxed, regulated—all to suit the needs of the elites who control our destiny. We have become a ship of fools, foundering in a sea of riches, while losing our freedom, our rights, and our futures.

TRUE CAPITALISM VERSUS CORRUPTED CAPITALISM

Just as there are the two forms of capitalism, there are two types of regulation. The debate is not simply a matter of being pro-regulation or anti-regulation. On the one hand, we must oppose regulations that restrict free markets, or allow cheating, such as monopolies, subsidies, costly licensing, or any artifice that reduces the equality and ethical behavior of participants. And, on the other hand, we need regulations that encourage new entrants, enable free and open competition, punish unethical business practices, and require full and honest financial reporting by all public businesses. Unless that distinction is honored, as Senator Warren has explained, true capitalism cannot flourish.

That is why recognizing that free people create strong economies is so important--it provides the standard by which to measure the value of any proposed regulation: the regulation must support widespread and equal participation and prevent unfair practices. That fact may come as a surprise because proper regulation of the economy is, in fact, that simple.

Economic policy is in truth so simple that elites have had to muddy the water to confuse the public. They may say that they agree regulations are stifling and then remove the regulations that stifle *their* behavior. But the whole purpose of good regulation must be to limit unfair practices and selfish interests! The continuing war that the ordinary people must fight is to preserve *inclusive* institutions and laws and prevent the elites from inserting *exclusive* regulations that give them a license to steal.

All that it would take would be some honest referees in the government departments charged with overseeing the economy. It's no different from a baseball game or a cricket match: you need clear rules and honest competent referees. Today's democracies have too many rules, ridden with loopholes and exceptions, all administered by too many corrupt referees!

Note that communism, socialism, and fascism are all "big-government" systems that over-regulate the economy. They are all mere variations of the failed mercantilist system. They are as a group, juxtaposed against the free and fair form of capitalism and have three things in common with each other:

1. They allow the elites at the top to manipulate rulemaking to their own advantage,

2. by granting the power of management to elites they create the problems of authoritarianism, corruption, unfairness, and inefficiency in government, and

3. they suppress their peoples' creativity and energy that would otherwise flourish in a free and open economy.

In brief, it is that curse of corruption, as well as the cost of a bloated and inefficient government, that clearly instructs us that "the best government is the one that governs the least." By their nature, governments tend to be heavy-handed and corrupt. They are a monopoly, with an unlimited power to tax, to prosecute their enemies, to suppress rebellion and protests, with little accountability or responsibility. Currently, they are enacting laws that dictate the mechanics of elections, and employing the power of the media, airwaves, and schools to support their evil designs. Anyone who wants to give elites more power and the government more control must be nuts!

HOW ELIZABETH WARREN WOULD "FIX" CAPITALISM

Ironically, it was a Democratic Senator from Massachusetts, often vilified as a "socialist," who clarified the issue over "capitalism." In an interview with Anand Giridharadas he asked her, "what if it is capitalism itself, its inherent logic, not the distortion of it, that is the problem behind this economy, this wealth disparity, this planetary emergency? What if it's a system that fundamentally elevates money, the pursuit of money, over the pursuit of all else?"

To Senator Warren's great credit, she replied:

"I don't see it that way. And let me try to explain just a little bit. I believe that, at its best, we have a system that works with markets, and markets can produce a lot of value, but only markets with rules. Markets without rules are theft. And so confusing markets without rules, markets that are not real competitive markets, with what passes for capitalism in many parts of the world today, is missing the central element. And the reason I think this is so important is that this is where we get into the discussion, for example, about socialism.

"So, what's your alternative to a market-based system? A system in which the government decides the allocation of goods and services? Because the problem you run into there is that the same bigotry and prejudice and lust for power that can infect a capitalist system can infect any other system as well.

"This is about the need for vigilance in our rules, why we need rules that are fair and that are consistently enforced. If we do that, markets will produce great value and great opportunity for our people. And if we don't have those rules, replacing the market part of the system is not going to help."[143]

Thus, Senator Warren makes the economic argument quite clear: Free markets and capitalism work well but the marketplace must be open to all, with no favoritism, and the rules ensuring fair competition must be enforced vigorously.

And she sums that up by arguing for a wealth tax and graduated income taxes on capital gains: "Let's change the rules on taxation and then aggressively enforce them and use the money that we get to expand opportunity. That's how we make real change...we have so under-taxed those at the top that it's had two consequences. One is that it's part of the reason they've been able to build such enormous fortunes, because wealth itself for this top group hasn't been taxed. But the second consequence is they then get to use it in ways they decide they want to use it. And last I saw, there aren't many billionaires making charitable contributions to enforce serious environmental regulations, to enforce serious anti-monopoly regulations, to put in place a well-funded enforcement agency to make certain that people aren't getting cheated on financial products."

Clearly, Warren supports capitalism and free markets and understands how elites have corrupted it to gain an advantage. The solution is to eliminate all the loopholes enjoyed by the ultra-wealthy, maintain a fair business climate, penalize those who cheat, and tax the huge fortunes amassed by the elites to reduce the growing disparity in wealth among American citizens. She thus makes a bold call for reforms which reveal a clear understanding of today's business world. Some of her welfare proposals may be questioned, but she is one of the few who understand the difference between true capitalism and the corrupted form that exists currently in most countries of the world.

THE FALSE LURE OF SOCIALISM

It is an undeniable fact that Karl Marx, Che Guevara, Norman Thomas, Fidel Castro, Leo Trotsky, Mao Tse Tung, Lenin, Stalin, and Bernie Sanders have all presented a believable case: That capitalism has shown an evil and despotic nature that has sometimes condemned the working masses to a life of harsh labor supporting the obvious greedy elites who exist like parasites on the sweat of the poor. However, those failings of capitalism develop only when elites have distorted the rules that must govern a free market. A free market must be refereed, just like a soccer match, to make sure that rules are honored and that no one cheats.

Senator Elizabeth Warren, a fierce critic of crony capitalism, did make clear who was to blame for making the very productive free market appear inadequate: "A lot of these (billionaires) are not capitalists. They're all for competitive markets for someone else, but they would like to live in an America where they're getting all of the tax breaks, where they're getting all of the subsidies, where their employees are supported through public dollars to pay for their healthcare and food and housing, and where the owners of these businesses don't have to pay a living wage."[144]

ON THE LURE OF SOCIALISM

"Any man who is not a socialist at age twenty has no heart, and any man who is still a socialist at forty has no brain."

~~FRENCH POLITICIAN CLEMENCEAU

Those criticisms of capitalism, which have considerable merit, where the elites have corrupted the marketplace, explain why so many long-suffering common people listen in awe to the seductive appeal that demagogues make--to rise-up, "throw off your chains," and demand the right to a fair share in the material bounty of their nation.

Further, what those rebellious leaders say about the arrogant and greedy elites living at the top of the pile, feasting off those below is, for the most part, spot on. However, one thing seems totally clear: Although all those advocates who pursue a socialist agenda are primarily correct in their complaints, they are equally wrong in their prescribed remedies. They make three mistakes in seeking a solution for the unjust systems that we all continue to endure:

> **First**, they blame free enterprise, with its open marketplace, for their sorrows, yet all the people living in such free markets have consistently enjoyed superior amounts of disposable income and a better standard of living.

Second, they look to socialism, with its necessarily bigger government, in the vain hope that it would fix their problems; a government that might provide them with more justice and greater opportunity. Sadly, it is the growth of big government that has corrupted the free marketplace and it is that corruption that is the source of their unhappiness. Making government bigger would only make matters worse.

Third, the best solution is to reject the false promises of help from the elites and demand that the government enforce rules that keep the marketplace open and fair and prevents unfair practices, selective subsidies, and favoritism.

The need to regulate the operation of the free market has always opened the door for its manipulation by those doing the regulating. Instead of acting as good referees, to ensure a fair playing field, government officials are too often tempted to use their power for personal gain. For example, politicians can threaten to impose harmful regulations on our businesses and trade unions or offer those groups advantages—anything they want, or don't want, is for sale.

Once the unions and corporatists know that government is for sale, *they* will approach the politicians and offer additional "contributions" in return for favored treatment. The result is that some of the biggest financial deals of today are being negotiated by politicians! Even worse, we know that foreign governments are now getting in on the deal-making. Some of our so-called leaders have recently received money in "pay-offs" from Russian, Ukrainian, and Chinese governments. How can we rely on such officials to protect America's interests when they are accepting bribes from our biggest international adversaries? Indeed, isn't the taking of bribes from other nations, especially enemy or rogue nations, a form of treason?

SUMMARY

This book is to designed to explain that it is *people* who build prosperous societies, how those successful nations have usually been corrupted by rulers, why that eternal battle between elites and the common people has played a dominant role in the Rise and Fall of Nations, and what we actually need to do is make sure that both our elections and our free markets operate fairly, not unfairly, and in no way helping the few who try to subvert the rules in their own favor. In short, government officials must accept their role as honest referees so that every citizen can exercise their genius and share its riches.

We do have regulations to minimize monopolistic and unfair trade practices, but we need honest officials to enforce them. And regulations that restrict new entrants or reduce fair competition must be removed. The major reason that such a proper balance of regulations has been difficult to maintain is that so many people want to gain an unfair advantage.

WHY CAPITALISM NEEDS HONEST REFEREES

Che Guevara stands tall
as a symbol of radical revolution for
those oppressed by
an unfair capitalistic society.
An angry man who had the right
complaints but the wrong solution!

The only effective solution is to maintain impartial and effective regulation that allows all participants easy access to enter the market, penalizes cheating, and breaks up the giant financial interests that lobby our lawgivers. It won't be easy but electing only the most honest and determined people to office would be a good start. Just because many in government are corrupt, and work against the people's interests, does not mean that such destructive actors cannot be removed by the voters.

The need to reduce corruption and look for and elect honest leaders is truly urgent; perhaps the most important factor in choosing who to vote for. A politician who promises that a bigger government will take care of the people, fully intends to use that more intrusive government to manage and oppress the people. Fidel Castro and Che Guevara illustrate this point: Making their government more powerful only made it more corrupt and authoritarian, a condition that caused its citizens to lose their unity and optimism. (As a Russian worker famously said, "the government pretends to pay us, and we pretend to work.") Without the support of their people, the Decline in both Cuba and Russia accelerated toward a final Collapse, the subject of the next chapter.

CHAPTER 12-

The Collapse of Nations: Elites at Work

 *"Why don't democracies work? Because they are only temporary states… They can only function until a majority of voters discover that they can vote themselves money and other goodies from the public treasury."*
~~Joseph Farah

O NCE THE CAUSE FOR A nation's Rise is established, it is easy to identify the causes of its eventual Fall. It's all about the people. If they set up good laws and institutions, they will do well. If after a time they let those supports deteriorate and allow elites to corrupt the political process and the free market, they and their country will then do poorly.

Niall Ferguson, in *The Great Degeneration*, asserts that our way of life is built on four institutional pillars: representative government, the free market, the rule of law, and civil society.

"It was these institutions, rather than any geographical or climatic advantage, that set the West on the path to prosperity and security." And he points to a deterioration in those institutions as the cause of America's slowing growth, crushing debts, increasing economic inequality, and antisocial behavior.[145]

This author would only add that the *key* pillar was *the people*; those who had the sense to establish and maintain the four supportive pillars that Ferguson lists. And it follows that if we the people allow those pillars to be undermined, then we will be to blame, and we will suffer from the resulting degeneration.

Ferguson quotes Adam Smith on the cause of such degeneration: "Laws and institutions degenerate to the point that elite rent-seeking dominates the economic and political process."[146] Ferguson illustrates this breakdown as how "public debt has become a way for the older generation to live at the expense of the young and unborn, regulation has become dysfunctional...lawyers...become parasites, and civil society withers..."[147] That condemnation of "elite rent-seeking" and "regulations becoming dysfunctional" are correct as far as they go, but the causes are not made clear by either writer. On the cover jacket of Ferguson's book, it is described as "an incisive indictment of an era of negligence and complacency," but note that the blame is aimed at "the era," not the actual guilty individuals—first, the elites who subverted the rules and institutions that had been helping the people at large, and second, the "negligent and complacent" people who stood by and allowed that subversion.

Alexander Deane makes a more pointed argument--he blames the victims, arguing that "our middle class has failed to uphold societal values, and the enormously damaging collapse of our society's norms and standards is largely a result of that abdication."[148] Deane, thus, takes the wise but hard-nosed tack that "people get the government they deserve!"

If you recognize that almost all elites will, sooner or later, seek to hog the community's abundance, then that "problem" coming from the elites is similar to those problems posed by geography, climate, and a lack of natural resources. The energetic people of free nations have always sought to overcome obstacles and we must accept the fact that one of the biggest obstacles that we face are the elites. Just as we must find cleaner and safer sources of energy, so must we find ways to harness our leaders so that instead of creating partisan strife and feeding their bank accounts they concentrate on our national interests, equality of opportunity, and preserving our personal liberty.

> "The art of nation-making, as of law-making and of institution-building generally, is the art of containing power and ambition so that they act for, rather than against, the common good."
>
> ~ IVO MOSLEY
> *IN THE NAME OF THE PEOPLE*

HOW VENICE'S GLORY FINALLY FADED

The collapse of Venice provides us with a perfect illustration of how elites eventually destroy great nations. Authors Acemoglu and Robinson make a strong argument that the Decline started when the elite gained the upper hand in the early fourteenth century. For hundreds of years the city's institutions had been reasonably inclusive and allowed upward mobility. Most important had been the development of a form of limited partnership business enterprise (The Commenda) where wealthy merchants would partner with young entrepreneurs to conduct trade.

Starting in the tenth century, these partnerships grew substantially, with the wealthy partner advancing most of the funds and sharing profits with an enterprising partner. This led to the elevation of many lower-status people into the higher financial circles. Government documents between 960 and 982 AD show that 65-81 percent of the names recorded were new names, not previously among the leading Venetians.[149] Those numbers indicate extensive upward mobility. During that period, there were many financial and legal innovations, and "the dynamic moving Venice toward fully inclusive institutions looked unstoppable."[150] Free enterprise and capitalism flourished.

However, the existing elites, fearing the growing competition from the increased upward mobility, brought proposals to the Great Council on October 3, 1286, to change the rules. It was defeated, but being brought again two days later was approved, and the entry of new successful entrepreneurs was made more difficult. During the next twelve years, membership became largely an inherited right for existing elite families. La Serrata (The Closure) of Venice had been accomplished. "The Great Council was now closed to outsiders, and the incumbents had become a hereditary aristocracy. The seal on this came in 1315, with the *Libro d'Oro*, or 'Gold Book,' which was an official registry of the Venetian nobility."[151]

Thomas Madden confirms that brief period when the elites gained control of Venice: "After 1323 it was possible for the Venetians to make a definitive list of those families with a right to membership in the Great Council...Venice, therefore, had legally defined the boundaries of a hereditary governing class."[152]

So, where were the people during this legal coup by the elites? They protested, so the elites expanded the Council, but kept majority control, and in 1310 established a police force for the first time and used it to punish protestors. Then they banned the use of Commenda contracts to block new merchants from entering the established commercial activities. In 1314 they nationalized trade by taking over shipping and regulating trade. After 1324 they imposed high taxes on any competing shipping.

Thus, in a twenty-eight-year period, from 1286 to 1314, the elites in effect undid 900 years of successful republican rule and closed the economic world to the common people. They did it simply by changing the rules governing politics and businesses. The process illustrates the close relationship between political freedom and economic freedom: The Venetian elites brought on the eventual collapse of their republic by gaining control of the political sphere and then using that power to limit the economic rights of their citizens.

"This was the beginning of the end of Venetian prosperity. Ordinary people began leaving the city. By 1500 the population had shrunk substantially.... Instead of pioneering trade routes and economic institutions, Venetians now make pizza and ice cream and blow colored glass for hordes of foreigners.... Venice went from economic powerhouse to museum."[153] And it was all caused by their elites who found ways to limit the activities of the common people. After the Serrata, with the people oppressed and leaving the region, the power of Venice gradually declined and in 1797 Napoleon's troops, with little resistance, moved in and occupied the city and its mainland territory.

THE COLLAPSE OF NATIONS

"A great civilization is not conquered from without until it has destroyed itself from within."

~~ARIEL DURANT

The story of that Most Serene City provides a clear picture of how free people can build a great nation and a vibrant economy by holding their leaders on a short leash, fully accountable to the people. It also shows how, in a moment of inattention, when the people are not watching, the elites can gain control, change the laws and institutions to their own benefit, and thereby bring on the inner decay that, unless reversed, will end in collapse.

That sudden turnaround in Venice, when elites finally gained dominance, bears a striking resemblance to the disruptive political scenario facing Americans in 2021: By hyping climate change, the Corona virus, and green energy imperatives, the elites have divided the people and distracted them from more vital issues. By using their monopoly control of public schools to teach critical race theory, a cancel culture-common core curricula, and our country's racist past, the elites are creating a citizenry passionately Anti-America. By enforcing federal mandates and politically correct speech they are training Americans to follow orders from above. And, by allowing massive immigration, and removing voter identification controls, the elites will be able to corrupt and control future elections.

The elite's greedy ambitions are culminating in a sudden grab for centralized power that rivals how the Venetian elite gained total control 700 years ago and how the Roman Republic was crushed more than 2000 years ago. Such tipping points have occurred before and will happen again. History tells us that free people, happily enjoying their families and homes, can quickly lose those rights, suddenly, permanently, and when least expected.

HOW THE ENLIGHTENMENT THINKERS MUDDIED THE WATERS

Fortunately, an American collapse into tyranny can be avoided. In 1997, Arthur Herman examined the obsession many historians have with the *idea* of Western Decline and exposed the folly of the doomsayers who assume every nation must fall. He suggests that the idea that democracies must eventually collapse is pure nonsense; there are no absolute rules governing the behavior of Homo sapiens.

It was the "great" Enlightenment thinkers who started this dismal outlook. Herman writes that "cultural pessimism draws heavily on the philosophy of Friedrich Nietzsche and on his sweeping condemnation of the European society of his day as sick and decadent.... (This) has become so pervasive that we accept it as a normal intellectual stance—even when it is contradicted by our own reality."[154] The reality was that in 1844, when Nietzsche was born in Germany, Europe was arguably the best place in the world for a baby to find itself. Flawed as those countries may have been, his ancestors had fashioned one of the most free and prosperous environments in the world. Indeed, it was that benign environment that gave Nietzsche the opportunity to reside in comfort at major universities where he could condemn the culture around him.

We should not condemn Nietzsche too much for that indolent sneer at his home country, because even in America today, many of our most educated citizens live in luxury, sneering at "Amerika's" culture, our low-class citizenry, while never even considering the idea of moving elsewhere. Denigrating everything around them is a common feature among intellectuals and some elites; it sustains their self-image of superiority and helps distinguish them as above the common people.

However, Nietzsche's most significant failings were his "suggestions" that we could make the world better by abolishing religion, helping the powerful crush weaker members of their communities, suppressing Judeo-Cristian morality, denying the existence of free will, and by identifying and praising the "supermen" who should rule over the common herd of inferior beings. One can safely wager that he would not have been a fan of George H. W. Bush's "thousand points of light" to make the community a kinder and gentler place for humans to enjoy!

One of the most absurd ideas of the Enlightenment philosophers was that "society" is comparable to a biological organism, like an apple tree or a goat, with a defined lifecycle. (How do they dream up this stuff?!) Once that false analogy was constructed, many other equally false conclusions followed. These brilliant thinkers claimed that nations followed the same predetermined lifecycle as donkeys! Do they know about China, Iran, and India? All struggling along, for better or worse, for more than 3,000 years!

Herman criticizes over a dozen of those Great Philosophers for this damaging obsession and points out that "a society's future is not the product of some inevitable law of Progress, or Decrepitude; it is what the society's members decide to make of it."[155] But today's experts, as cultural pessimists, avoid discussing such individual action, and instead base their thinking on the false assumption "that individuals have significance only if they are part of a larger whole."[156]

However, the error in such thinking is self-evident—great and historic individuals like Rosa Parks, Alfred Einstein, Winston Churchill, and Abraham Lincoln marched to their own drummer. Their significance was self-made, not from being part of some group! Lincoln grew up in a rural homestead, started work as a rail splitter, and enjoyed dirty jokes. If ever there was an "original" it was Lincoln! And yet he was a key figure in ending slavery in America! Thus, we are reminded that the ordinary individuals of this world get no respect from many of the best and brightest!

Herman's respect for individual action is clear; he asserts, "The most characteristic product of the Western humanist tradition is the free and autonomous individual—who is also the cultural pessimist's worst enemy."[157] That "autonomous individual," we must emphasize, is also the elite's worst enemy for he or she stands in their way to power and control.

Herman makes it very clear that the great democracies of history were built by individual people and maintained by the supportive institutions constructed "by (those) individuals acting in concert. Race, class, and gender do not in fact determine the direction of society and history.... The real forces for change lie in the choices we make as individuals, the actions they set in motion, and their consequences for others."[158]

In brief, Herman comes close to the theme of this book: People have gradually, over thousands of years, gained rights and vibrant economies but only through their own implacable insistence. And, as we were all taught until half a century ago, we did it by hoisting ourselves up by our own bootstraps! And for almost 400 years, until just recently, nobody had the gall to tell them that the government had done it for them! That is why only the American people can save us from losing our liberty. Never forget that the reason elites love Big Government is that a Leviathan bureaucracy reduces the people's liberty and grants rulers more power.

INSTITUTIONS - BOTH GOOD ONES AND BAD ONES - ARE DESIGNED BY PEOPLE

Many historians point to collapsing laws and institutions as the cause of national decline, but how can they "collapse?" If those institutions have worked, why would anyone want to change them? Sure, small adjustments might be useful to let them function better, but why would anyone want to alter institutions that worked well to help the people?

ON BANK BAILOUTS

"Capitalism without bankruptcies is like Christianity without Hell."

~ JOHAN NORBERG, FINANCIAL FIASCO

It's not rocket science. Obviously, corrupt self-aggrandizing people will always want to change the rules to help make *their* lives better, even at the expense of all the other people. In Chapter 11, we saw how a few wealthy bankers in 1910 created the federal reserve system that gave the major banks control over the economy and an advantage over the smaller "country" banks. That allowed the fox to guard the hen house and has not worked well; within 20 years the excess power gained by Wall Street banks and the excess exuberance of its speculators helped bring on the Great Depression.

The resulting widespread misery of the early 1930s prompted President Franklin Roosevelt, FDR, to ask Joe Kennedy to break up the rogue financial institutions on Wall Street. As Chairman of the SEC and with the newly adopted regulations of the Glass-Steagall Act, Kennedy quickly ended the self-dealing activities of banks, brokers, and security underwriters. Those three financial groups could no longer act as collaborators controlling Wall Street and the market for securities.

Fast forward to 1999, and we see that the financial and banking elites got Congress to pass a law eliminating that Glass-Steagall Act, which had helped regulate the financial elites for more than sixty years. It was a bi-partisan gift to the bankers. A Republican controlled Congress passed the bill and President Clinton, a Democrat, signed it into law. Then, Clinton's successor, President George W. Bush, encouraged new lower standards for home mortgages. For the next seven years sub-prime mortgages were handed out to all borrowers on a silver platter. It was a bi-partisan endeavor! And the bankers and mortgage brokers made a fortune!

Predictably, that loosening of standards enriched the bankers but ended in 2008 with a crash that broke many homeowners. Clearly, the crooks had again been set loose in the hen house. Those changes to the law helped the wealthy Wall Street elites but led directly to a boom-and-bust scenario, and the 2008 banking collapse that wiped out the savings of many middle-class Americans. That was a real-world example of *How Institutions Decay and Economies Die*, which is the subtitle to Ferguson's book.

It was not hard to predict that when Congress voided the Glass-Steagall Act the bankers would gain a clear path to increased profits— they were paid large fees and bonuses for bundling the bum bonds for sale to the public and calling them "safe" investments. The rating companies such as Moody's and Standard & Poor's kept giving "A" ratings to the risky securities and thereby failed to warn the public. Politically appointed officials at Fannie Mae and even the Securities Exchange Commission joined the cabal, ignoring the risks and guaranteeing the product with the public's money.

When it all collapsed, the executive branch, with the approval of Congress, bailed out the bankers. The problem was not the "decay" of institutions; the problem was that elites changed the laws to help themselves. In this case, the benefits all went to the executives at the large financial institutions and Fannie Mae who walked away with undeserved fees and bonuses. Homeowners are still reeling from the huge losses they suffered. Few economists had pointed out the danger. And the politicians and media buried the truth, and nobody went to jail.[159]

Christopher Hayes has pointedly asked, "Are economists who publish papers praising financial deregulation giving us an honest assessment…or courting extremely lucrative consulting fees from banks?"[160] His book details how extreme income inequality has combined with a new "Cult of Smartness" to create an elite, especially, in the financial sector of the economy, that is out of touch with average Americans, more ethically challenged, with a greater feeling of entitlement, and most rewarded with influence. Hayes concludes, "We can't be sure, in short, just who our elites are working for. But we suspect it is not us."[161]

That 2008 mortgage meltdown was a classic example of what happens when greedy elites succeed in changing good laws and institutions so they can profit: They get richer, the rest get poorer, and the country suffers—one more example of how true and "honest" capitalism is being twisted into crony capitalism. That's why the elites are compared to *parasites*! It is a massive mismatch; the elites usually end up winning, the nation declining, and the people suffering.

TWISTING TRUE CAPITALISM INTO CRONY CAPITALISM

Parasitic elites have always had trouble infiltrating successful free market democracies. The biggest obstacle they face is the open marketplace with its countervailing forces, large independent businesses, and a self-reliant middle class. However, once elites get the power to regulate, educate, and tax those groups, they control them. The battle for control pits the elites against any form of true capitalism where everyone participates on an equal basis. Their battle for control also pits them against "democracy" where the government works <u>for</u> the people. Their goal is simply to twist the rules so they can benefit from the same form of favoritism that was the failing of mercantilism.

Wall Street has...forged a partnership with Washington elite giving Wall Street almost unlimited powers and opportunities to destroy the American dream... when government and bankers operate as one, the middle class loses.

MARK MULLEN,
WHO CONTROLS AMERICA, 67-8

Christopher Hayes has pointed out that the failings of corrupt capitalism may be alleviated by redistribution but that it is wiser to remove the causes:

"The most pressing challenge for those who desire a better functioning more representative nation is conceiving not of policies that will ultimately enhance equality but of mechanisms by which the power of the current elite might be dramatically reduced,"[162]

Thus, Hayes confirms that it is a mistake to look to government redistribution of wealth as a remedy. First, any distribution requires administrators in government to do the distribution and that breeds dependency in the recipients and corruption among the administrators. How can any nation succeed if it is run by corrupt leaders who patronize dependent citizens? No thank you! Redistribution is good for assisting the truly needy, but the able bodies need a level playing field, an honest government, fair play, and the liberty to make whatever they want out of their lives.

In essence, the elites have rigged the rules, making their share of national income and wealth too much greater than everyone else's, and now argue that they need more power to fix everything. Few people understand that the elites caused those problems, they created the disparities in wealth, and are primarily intent on making the disparities even bigger.

WHY UNITY, PRIDE, AND ATTITUDE MATTER

History has shown that the people of mature nations tend to lose their energy and spirit. New restrictions, reduced opportunities, violent demonstrations, partisan bickering, and burdensome taxes eventually suck the joy out of their lives. The bureaucracy wears them down; eventually, optimism turns into weariness. It then becomes easier for elites to seduce voters into falling in line with the elites' objectives.

The elites understand all those tricks: they use the schools to shape the peoples' attitudes and beliefs, undermine patriotism, faith, families, and the hope of upward mobility. Gradually they find ways to change a moral self-reliant population into a dependent and apathetic mass. They do that to gain control, but the result is to destroy the source of the nation's strength—Its people. That cycle has been seen throughout history; the elites never rest from their efforts to get control and enrich themselves.

Alexander Fraser Tytler in 1787, almost 250 years ago, drew his "Dismal Circle" that shows the life of every democracy as having nine stages. They start with a group of people who primarily have a self-reliant, optimistic, and moral belief system, then gradually become materialistic, gradually grow complacent, then fall into dependency, and ending in Bondage, the ninth and final stage before Collapse. At that terminal point, having lost the energy of a unified and enterprising people, the nation gradually falls into obscurity.

Regrettably, it appears that many of the people in the Western democracies are currently well along to the complacent and dependent stages. That gradual advance from self-reliance and optimism to an attitude of apathy and dependency is largely caused by the gradual increase in power of the nation's elites. Starting as an egalitarian community, elites corrupt the marketplace, impose restrictions on the people, use the schools to condition the youth, and tilt the laws and tax policies to enrich themselves. Faced with an unfair situation, with the deck stacked against them, many citizens lose their initiative and drift toward apathy and dependency. The ancient Roman elites used "bread and circuses" to calm the masses as their leaders took more and more of the abundance. Today, they use generous payouts from the federal government, already ballooning the national debt to astronomical levels. And, more ominously, the elites are now using Orwellian techniques such as Politically Correct speech mandates, forced vaccinations, and brainwashing methods in the schools. It is no longer possible to ridicule The Brave New World of Aldous Huxley, complete with biological controls and lobotomies, and a "bee-hive" structure of enslaved workers providing for a leadership class. When I first read Huxley's book, more than half a century ago, its dystopian world seemed rather far-fetched, but, unfortunately, subsequent developments are making its possibility more believable.

The following quote is often attributed to Tytler: "A democracy is always temporary in nature; it simply cannot exist as a permanent form of government. A democracy will continue to exist up until the time that voters discover that they can vote themselves generous gifts from the public treasury. From that moment on, the majority always votes for the candidates who promise the most benefits from the public treasury, with the result that every democracy will finally collapse due to loose fiscal policy, which is always followed by a dictatorship."

Tytler was one of the great "common sense" philosophers in Scotland, and like his countrymen Thomas Reid, John Witherspoon, and Francis Hutchinson, his ideas resonated in the minds of practical Americans as they devised a constitution with checks and balances. America's founders were not concerned with natural resources, climate, or waterways. Like Tytler, they were concerned about the attitudes and liberty of their people. It is those attitudes and self-reliance that the elites are trying to destroy in order to gain their selfish objectives.

When our elites disparage America, remember that they do not do that out of respect or tolerance for other nations or cultures. When they denigrate religion and patriotism, they are not trying to help our people. When our kids are taught in their classrooms that America's past is evil, the "educators" are not trying to help the average American. Our elites are neither kind nor generous. They are impatient to get around to Tytler's end stages. They get there by destroying our pride, our families, and our patriotism. Creating disunity, discontent, and despair is the elite's way of getting ahead of the common herd—Us!

For those working full-time, struggling to pay their bills, it is almost inevitable that some will become apathetic just as predicted in the final stages of Tytler's Dismal Circle. Then, without their contribution, the society is bound to decline. The final Fall is rarely caused by environmental degradation, the climate, or a lack of resources. People, certain kinds of people, cause nations to decline.

SUMMARY

We must accept the fact that some humans will always try to bend the rules and spoil everything. All citizens in a democracy must be vigilant to prevent rulebreakers from gaining power. If we watched our politicians as closely as we watch our NBA games, they would certainly be forced to act more honorably.

BEWARE: The people you elect will not always be working for you. Until they restore integrity to our business place and our state and national governments, and reduce the extreme inequalities of wealth, they are working for the elites. When they take money from foreign governments they are working against America's interest. As long as they apply more lenient standards of justice on their cronies than on you, they are not working for you. As long as they avoid teaching useful tools for personal success to our school children, they are not working for us. Indeed, when have they ever worked for us?!

Integrity in Washington will not just somehow make a magical appearance! Politicians are very good at describing attractive policies. They are at the top of their game when they describe policies that they have no intention of fulfilling! Don't take their promises seriously. They rarely come to fruition, and when they do, they often do more harm than good!

Remember that the job of elected officials is primarily to manage our huge government efficiently and honestly. That requires us to put honesty as the number one qualification and experienced management competency second.

SUMMARY OF PART III

Irreconcilable Differences: The Elites Versus the Common People

During the last 200 years it has become undeniable that people on every continent are equally capable at building prosperous nations. In fact, the extent of their prosperity appears to vary directly with the degree of freedom enjoyed. Free economies are springing up all around the world, as documented by the Several Annual Indices of Economic Freedom.

However, elites are not team players; they hate free economies; they just want a bigger share of their nation's wealth. To hold onto power, they corrupt the free market, denigrate family and faith, undermine self-reliance, create tax and regulatory obstacles for others, provide loopholes for themselves, and divide the people into warring groups. Then, pointing at all the inequities (that they created), they claim that they can make everything better!

Elites gain their power by eviscerating the unity, morale, and energy of the people. They do it to gain control. The solution is to recognize that the common people are our prime asset so we must vote to elect candidates who will restore a truly representative government, an open and free market, an even application of the rule of law, and a civil society.

THE PARASITIC ROLE OF ELITES

PART IV

Winning the War by Expanding Freedom
(2000 AD - 2050 AD)

CHAPTER 13-

Ways of Thinking -- Abstract vs. Concrete

 These (common) people…ask no questions;
they live, seemingly, for the day, they waste
no energy or substance on the effort to
understand life; they enjoy the physical experience of living…
If they are wise, surely the rest of us are fools.
George F. Kennan

PREVIOUS CHAPTERS HAVE SUMMARIZED THE accumulating innovations and open economies that spread throughout Europe in the Middle Ages. The people who forged that progress spent their time working with and developing labor saving devices. They had little use for abstract theories. They were grounded in everyday problems and looked for better ways of accomplishing more tasks. That is why they devised the innovative technologies that shook up the rigid Medieval cultures and liberated mankind from the most arduous labor. Professor E. L. Jones has pointed out that most of their technical advances were not huge steps forward, but came from "ceaseless tinkering," as "stages in a continual evolution," a constant "secretion of little details."[163]

Although Professor Jones makes no reference to who did all that vital "tinkering," it is obvious that those many baby steps were the work of thousands of mechanics and engineers who built labor saving devices, starting in ancient times with the primitive wheel, gears, and pulleys and advancing to the complex machines that powered the Industrial Revolution. And it has been the same class of people who have recently moved on to mastering artificial intelligence, quantum physics, and interplanetary travel.

Those practical individuals stand in stark contrast to those whom Thomas Sowell has described as the "soft-scientists" who tend to lean toward the "doomsday" crowd. The latter group are constantly alarming everyone with their fears for the future; fears that are often based only on theoretical and uncertain possibilities. Because they have little experience in solving problems, they overestimate them. In the more dramatic personalities, they may even imagine the imminent total annihilation of the human race. Christopher Hayes has warned us about those "smart" people:

"Extreme intelligence…without sufficient wisdom, judgment, empathy, and ethical rigor… can be extremely destructive… This dynamic in which the smart, sneering, self-assured hawk steamrolls his ideological opponents, should be well familiar to anyone who watched the run-up to the Iraq War. One of the great mysteries of the last two decades is how so many smart people could end up endorsing an idea as stupidly destructive as the Bush administration's war on Iraq."[164]

Hayes points out that "Behind many of the Bush administration's most disastrous and destructive decisions was one man: David Addington… Coworkers referred to him as 'extremely smart" and "sublimely brilliant."[165] And we all have heard of the two "whiz kids," McGeorge Bundy and Robert McNamara, who kept assuring Americans that we were winning the Vietnam War!

Curiously, these brilliant thinkers are often the more educated and articulate; they present simple but definitive prognostications, and then stick to their theories even if they keep failing. The practical individuals, often less educated but wiser and more skilled, know how to look for a solution and stand ready to adapt their efforts as needed. Thus, highly educated folks may be "smarter" but are not necessarily "wiser" than the less educated and are therefore frequently less reliable in their opinions. One writer has even suggested that their "misconceptions" arise from "a mind afflicted with madness."[166]

Ben Carson

"Like Karl Marx, today's political leaders believe...we are simply not smart enough to understand what is "good" for us."

BEN CARSON

After all, it was the soft-science experts and intellectuals who kept predicting that America would soon win the Vietnam War, that Russia's seventy-year economic experiment with communism would succeed, and that we would run out of oil. It is notable that all the innovations in energy during the last 100 years (from wood, 1920s; to coal, 1930s; to oil, 1940s; to nuclear, 1960s; to electric, 1980s; to solar and wind, 2000s) came from either ordinary workers or the physical scientists, never from the efforts of soft-science intellectuals, most of whom could never cut and split a cord of firewood, rig a turbine to a waterfall, or figure out the intricacies of the atom.

THE BATTLE OVER IDEOLOGIES

Despite the successful record of practical people using common sense to create efficient and prosperous nations, the intellectuals and academics have shaped our political debate into one about ideologies. Mark Bauerlein has pointed out the folly of such abstractions in an essay.[167] Intellectuals of both political parties cannot avoid that; that is how their minds function. They may be found expounding their theories in every political sphere, from the extreme Right to the far Left, and some make brilliant arguments, but few agree on anything. Many even reverse their ideological opinions in mid-life, vigorously opposing the ideas they had championed earlier!

Abstract thinkers "are very comfortable bouncing ideas around, and that extraordinary ability to manipulate the reasoning process leads them to love and promote all sorts of ideologies."[168] Their weakness is that they reduce everything to abstract concepts, often avoiding the obvious realities of political and social life. But there is nothing theoretical about creating free and open societies. The blueprint is there for all to see and emulate. It has been developed painstakingly by trial and error by common working people.

Right on the internet, you can download all the pre-printed forms for statutes, contracts, leases, licenses, deeds, mortgages, wills, trusts, corporate by-laws, incorporation documents, minutes of meetings, financial releases and discharges, and even Constitutions—you name it; they are all readily available. You might want a lawyer to help but all the mechanics for free business operations are there for the taking—no theories needed.

FREEDOM OPENS MANY MINDS
OPPRESSION CLOSES MINDS

"It cannot be emphasized too strongly that 'technological advance' does not mean only science; scientific geniuses are just one part of the knowledge process. Much technological advance comes from people who are neither well educated nor well paid..."

~ JULIAN SIMON

Soft scientists, who pretend that their field is a "science," have tried to embellish their work by using computer models and statistical analysis to support their theoretical "discoveries." However, since the prime actors in all economic activity are human beings, they are not as predictable as the atoms and electrons measured by the physical scientists. Consequently, those who study such subjects as politics, history, and economics, must rely on "estimates" and "assumptions" about how humans will behave. If any of those inputs are faulty, their models will prove useless for any practical purpose. Too often their results are just, "garbage in, garbage out!" And it is well known that some of them cherry pick the data they enter to gain the result they desire!

This subject was addressed by Kurt Vonnegut in his futuristic novel *Galapagos*, where we learn that the human race was wiped out simply because their brains had gotten too big; their thinking got so convoluted that they could no longer deal effectively with reality:

"The big problem wasn't insanity,

but that people's brains were much too big and

untruthful to be practical."[169]

As a brilliant satirist, Vonnegut was thus exposing the underlying problem Americans face: The reasoning power of too many of our elites, even those with good intentions, is deeply flawed. They themselves may well be a bigger threat than those dangers that they warn us about!

ABSTRACT THINKING VS. CONCRETE THINKING

In his books about self-made millionaires,[170] Thomas J. Stanley demonstrates that being *smart* has its limitations. People who are persistent, resilient, and flexible have often accomplished great goals, while the merely smart people have often made unwise decisions. His books document how "B" and "C" students have started most business enterprises in America, created the jobs that provide employment, and how they represent a large portion of the country's self-made millionaires.

The essence of it all is that in dealing with the reality of the world, a person needs a variety of personal traits other than sheer abstract and conceptual agility. And, in the soft sciences, excess reliance on abstractions can get in the way of wise practical solutions and become a handicap.

The major problem with very smart people is that they have been led to believe that their minds can solve all problems, not by inventing an actual new technological process, but by sheer reasoning with no hands-on work required. That helps explain why they propose theories on how a government can, merely by its "policies," overcome all the problems of their citizens.

Because they have gained power in most modern nations, their actions have greatly increased the size of governments. But the horrors of war and poverty have not lessened from that enormous growth of the governments. In fact, larger governments have added to the people's problems. John W. Danford has described those adverse trends of the twentieth century: "The state was the great gainer of the twentieth century and the central failure. Up to 1914, it was rare for the public sector to embrace more than 10% of the economy; by the 1970s... the state took 45 percent of the GNP."[171]

Thus, the private sector's share went down from 90 percent to 55 percent. If government had stayed fixed, the private sector would now enjoy (35/55ths) 63 percent more of the economy. In short, the growth of government has cut the working family's share of the nation's wealth almost in half. That is why it currently requires two workers per family to end up with the same spending power that one of their grandparents brought home. And it explains how the wealthy now have gained a far greater share of the nation's wealth than ever before. The top 10 percent have increased their share of the nation's wealth from 60 percent to 70 percent since the early 1980s, and the bottom 90 percent have seen their share go down from 40 percent to 30 percent.[172]

There is no mystery as to how this happened: The individuals directing our state and federal governments did it! It was the country's elites—the academics, Congress, politicians, CEO's, pundits, and lobbyists. And we the people acquiesced to it, and many still accept the elite's promises that they will create a better future—but we will probably get just more of the same. A simple projection indicates that our great-grandchildren will need three working members for each family—if "families" still exist.

THE DISMAL SCIENCE IS NOT SCIENTIFIC

Danford suggests that the hope that government could improve our lives "almost certainly was related to an excessive faith in the power of social sciences. The clearest case is the science of economics (which) persuaded generations of scholars and politicians that wise human beings, with the right information, could 'fine-tune' economic arrangements through government policies and central banking decisions, and thus improve the lives of human beings."[173] That hope might conceivably be brought to fruition if there were wise and honest human beings in charge of the process. However, as we have shown in this book, the human beings in charge almost always just want to use such tools to improve their own lives. And that has been the record for a long time. Certainly, the cyclical pattern of booms, busts, and bailouts has not been reduced by their attempts to "manage" the economy.

The social scientists who supported such governmental efforts can, in fact, "be identified as a source of the ills of free societies...there can be little doubt that social science has contributed to the increasingly widespread view that human beings are not fully responsible—perhaps scarcely responsible at all—for their actions."[174] This concept has fostered a dangerous belief that we should excuse bad behavior, that crime is the result of poverty, and that most everybody is a victim in need of government assistance.

IS A LIBERAL MIND DIFFERENT THAN A CONSERVA-TIVE'S MIND?

Anthony Walsh has observed that America is deeply divided, its people no longer "an aspirational melting pot of immigrants (but) more a salad bowl (of) … clashing flavors. Taking inspiration from

Coleridge's belief that all humans are temperamentally destined to follow the path of Plato the Idealist or Aristotle the Realist, Walsh's book[175] examines the political divide in terms of such temperamental differences: one group seeks to steer the nation sharply to the left into an egalitarian paradise, whereas the other side prefers an open economy to maintain a free and prosperous America.

Walsh's idea that the political divide is a function of different temperaments was presaged in Thomas Sowell's *A Conflict of Visions*, which suggests that conflicts about politics have existed for centuries and show a remarkably consistent pattern. Sowell distinguishes between those with a "constrained" vision, which sees human nature as enduring and self-centered, and the "unconstrained" vision, in which human nature is assumed to be perfectible. Those books offer a compelling case that the two opposing visions are behind our ideological disputes of whether human beings can ever be made uniformly "perfect.".

THE SEDUCTIVE LURE OF SOCIALISM

"Ideas that claimed to transcend all problems, but were defective or delusive, devastated minds, and movements, and whole countries, and looked like plausible contenders for world supremacy. In fact, humanity has been savaged and trampled by rogue ideologies."

—ROBERT CONQUEST
THE RAVAGED CENTURY

Sowell's opinion on the matter is made clear in just the title of another of his books: *Is Reality Optional?* Most people know that simple logic requires us to accept the realities of human nature. Common sense provides most people with a skeptical, or constrained view. Such people accept the fact that a large number of our fellow human beings will never be saints, that not everyone will be hard-working, honest, moral, or compassionate. Unfortunately, many people prefer to ignore reality and will embrace an unconstrained view because that opens up all sorts of pleasant scenarios and makes them feel good.

Voters who are attracted to seemingly kind policies, even when they are unrealistic, obviously think in an abstract way, as compared to concrete or practical thinkers. The former will often vote for a candidate simply because he or she makes the most appealing promises to help people. Thus, they serve as ardent supporters of smooth-talking elites who, in fact, may care zilch about such abstractions and simply want to gain the power to rule over all the people.

A voter's desire to feel good about themselves may even lead them to support a candidate who advocates impossible scenarios. Bryan Caplan's book, *The Myth of the Rational Voter: Why Democracies Choose Bad Policies,* explores these issues very well and recommends that our schools should put more emphasis on logic and rational thinking. However, that is not about to happen; our elites do not want to graduate logical and rational adults.

To illustrate that situation, I was recently engaged in a conversation with a granddaughter who had come to believe that Buddhism is far superior to Christianity. She cited the past sins of the Church and asked, "Why can't everyone just be nice?" Now she has received top grades in some of the best schools and colleges but is parroting the utopian dream, the unconstrained view, that people are malleable, perfectible, and therefore that all people should and could be "nice." She has been taught to set aside Charles Manson, Adolf Hitler,

Jack the Ripper, Pol Pot, and Josef Stalin, and enter a dream world of peace and calm where no one rocks the boat, and everyone is a "saint." Regrettably, it has been that type of wishful thinking that has made Buddhism a useful support for elites: Buddhists have rarely picked up clubs and pitchforks to demand equal rights.

I did my best to explain that many Homo sapiens will never attain a respectable level of "niceness;" that there are many selfish, aggressive, and even cruel people among us; and to think otherwise is to deny reality. Indeed, avoiding reality is what lazy people do to avoid the hard work of dealing with evil. I added that the Eastern Faiths, emphasizing passivity, "contemplating their navels," and never rocking the boat lest in their afterlife they might come back as a snake, was not only a denial of reality, but one of the reasons why those cultures did not progress as far as the Western democracies.

Seeing her eyes glaze over, apparently unable to evaluate such new and complicated thoughts, I didn't even try to point out that the Far Eastern potentates must have encouraged such passivity and acceptance among their people because it allowed them a freer rein to dominate and rule in peace, with less cantankerous citizens.

One might think that only a confused mind would fight for ideas that are supported only by noble intentions and unpredictable results. But the people who advocate for unrealistic programs aren't stupid! So how do you explain it? Scott Adams, creator of the satirical Dilbert cartoons, has provided the answer:

> "Politicians understand that reason will never have much of a role in voting decisions. A lie that makes a voter feel good is more effective than a hundred rational arguments. That's even true when the voter knows the

lie is a lie…. It makes people feel good about themselves when they support a supposedly charitable cause."[176]

A logical person may find such mental gymnastics incredible, but Adams warns that if you don't accept the fact that many people are irrational you will be hard-pressed to function in life! Perhaps that explains why would-be demagogues can confidently rely on the support of what Josef Stalin considered his "useful idiots." That is why politicians encourage "feel-good" policies--to get elected, sell books, and conform to the latest PC. They know that there are people who support unrealistic policies merely to gain, in Eric Voegelin's words, "a measure of gratification."[177] Those people serve as double idiots: first, by helping the crooks and opportunists, and second, by corrupting their own logic just to feel noble. Unfortunately, that type of failed reasoning is what our youth are being taught in today's schools. Bryan Caplan's compelling thesis about irrational voters results more from the indoctrination by our schools and media than from any lack of brain power.

BEAUTIFUL SEDUCTIVE LIES

"I needed to believe in a utopian vision of the future…. And I still need that belief, even if the particular vision I had embraced has turned to ashes."

GERDA LERNER, FIREWEED

The problem America faces is that it is the primarily abstract thinking members of the country that have become the movers and shakers among our elites and opinion leaders. Elites rely on them to complicate all matters of government and economics so no one can comprehend what is really going on. However, their ability to score well on tests guarantees admission to the "best" schools and colleges, and into the most prestigious and lucrative jobs. And their complex reasoning provides perfect cover for elites to juggle the laws and economy for their own gain.

We do know that the details of government and fair marketplaces are easily understood and that the complicated approaches argued over by economists and academics has done more harm than good. And it is certainly not clear if that type of abstract thinking has helped in governing the political and social affairs of nations. "Ancient Rome and Greece had some extraordinary leaders. If we compare today's leadership elite to the leaders of such ancient Republics, we can only conclude that progress has eluded twenty centuries of soft-science intellectuals."[178]

CHAPTER 14-

Micro-Finance: Economics Is Simple; No Theories Needed

"Increasing access to mobile (internet) services in Ghana has fostered the creation of business incubators.... The Meltwater School of Technology (MEST) teaches skills to help entrepreneurial young people...break into the software business...."

Brigit Helms
Access for All: Building Inclusive Financial Systems

If there is anything that illustrates how simple business and economics really are, it can be found in the sphere of micro-finance. For example, a few non-governmental organizations have made loans as small as a couple hundred dollars, with no collateral, to many impoverished individuals living in autocratic nations, and thereby provided the opportunity for them to do such simple things as obtain a pushcart to sell sandwiches.

That may seem a trifling amount, and a very insignificant transaction, but in fact it transforms that person into an independent self-employed individual, with an income, and the dignity and self-respect that comes from earning their own way.

MICRO-ECONOMICS

"The most important element is the micro-economic measures to promote and protect property rights, facilitate access to business transactions between individuals, and give people the necessary confidence to save, invest, and produce.... [Without those features] any macro-economic policy or external financing will be so much wasted effort."

~ HERNANDO DE SOTO

For an impoverished and oppressed person, that is a huge transformation. And when it's repeated for millions of such people, their nation feels the effect, and its people get to see the opportunity of freedom and the security that comes from taking advantage of economic opportunity. That power to improve the life of an average person, lifting them up from a beggar to a business owner, reveals the incredible contribution of free entrepreneurial economies. It is a shame that our State Department has little regard for such activities and instead gives billions of dollars to the leaders of those countries.

THE GRAMEEN BANK

The miracle of micro-finance got a boost on October 2, 1983, when the Bangladesh government licensed the Grameen Bank as an independent bank, formalizing the work of Muhammad Yunus in a Rural Economics Project he had conducted at Bangladesh's University of Chittagong. The bank was known as the "Bank of the Villages" in the Bengali language.

The Grameen Bank is not a very complicated institution. Professor Yunus simply believed that even in an impoverished country with few opportunities for its people, a small bank could provide loans, and a little coaching that would transform poor, helpless individuals into self-reliant entrepreneurs. His principles were used to organize loan applicants into small groups where each member would receive cash to create some form of self-employment. But Grameen did much more than merely lend its clients some money: The recipients had to agree to repay the loans, monitor each other, and coached by local Grameen agents, live by four principles: discipline, unity, courage, and hard work.

Grameen thus became a combination bank, a friendly priest, and a dedicated teacher, showing each applicant how to gain the respect due to a small, self-reliant businessman or businesswoman. And there were plenty of willing and able applicants: As of January 2011, the bank had 8.4 million borrowers, 97 percent of whom were women, and the repayment record was consistently over 90 percent. Grameen Bank is even expanding into wealthy countries, and in 2017, Grameen America had nineteen branches in eleven US cities.

The people in the poorest nations and cities appear to have no difficulty operating as entrepreneurs in the marketplace even when enabling institutional supports and protections are missing, as long as they get a little coaching, a small loan, and some encouragement.

THE WOMEN'S WORLD BANK

Another effort to alleviate poverty in the poorest nations was initiated during the first United Nations World Conference on Women in Mexico City in 1975. Esther Afua Ocloo was present, and as a Ghanaian entrepreneur, she already understood the importance of empowering would-be businesswomen. The following year, she became one of the founders of Women's World Banking, along with Michaela Walsh and Ela Bhatt, with Ocloo serving as its first chair of trustees.

Esther Ocloo, a blacksmith's daughter, born in Ghana, became an entrepreneur and then financed and coached millions of African women into businesses of their own.

Esther Ocloo is a prime example of how ordinary people make successful nations. She was born in the Volta Region to George Nkulenu, a blacksmith, and his wife Georgina, a potter and farmer, both of the Ewe people. Sent by her grandmother to a Presbyterian primary school, she advanced to a coeducational boarding school at Peki Blengo. After her schooling, she became the first person to start a formal food processing business in the Gold Coast, building her own business supplying marmalade and orange juice to the Achimota School.

Ms Ocloo went on to visit and study in England from 1949 to 1951 and studied at the post-graduate Food Preservation Course at Bristol University. When she returned to Ghana, she worked at expanding her business. It is safe to say that there are similar extraordinary individuals growing up in every nation of the world, possessing similar incredible self-reliance and initiative, just waiting for the opportunity to exert their genius, and all they need is a little encouragement and the freedom to do so.

In 1991, Nancy Barry took over the presidency and led the expansion of their network to include major banks, recognizing their potential to be innovative in bringing financial services to poor populations. During Barry's tenure, the WWB network grew to reach nearly twenty million low-income entrepreneurs. We should all ask, "Is there any one in our State Department who can claim any such valuable contribution to the people of the world?"

THE IMPACT OF SELF-SUFFICIENT PEOPLE

WWB's current president and CEO, Mary Ellen Iskenderian, took over leadership of the network in 2006. The WWB network currently serves twenty-four million micro-entrepreneurs in twenty-eight countries. The leaders of the organization have observed that the results of their individual transactions may appear small but that they have a significance far beyond the mere hundreds of dollars involved. Just making an improvement in a home, going from a mud floor to a wood floor, or from a cardboard roof to a metal one or allowing an additional year of schooling for a girl will have an enormous effect on a people accustomed to total stagnation.

Such small improvements are not a quick fix for poverty, but the access to financial services brings a measure of stabilization to the otherwise precarious lives of the poor. And the cumulative impact over years and in many households can be significant both in the comfort provided and, more importantly, by its positive effect on the attitude of the people. In a Forbes.com article, Mary Ellen Iskenderian stated that women's empowerment is hard to measure but that a boost in the attitude of an impoverished person is just as important as the economic benefits. It is important to understand "the tremendous potential that an institution…willing to work at the base of the pyramid could have on changing people's lives."[179]

Even without support from governments, the efforts of micro-finance organizations over the last fifty years have been remarkable. And currently, the Internet is helping expand the knowledge and ability of all connected people to participate in the ever-expanding world of business. Brigit Helms, in her book *Access for All: Building Inclusive Financial Systems*, writes: "The good news is that the past quarter century has ushered more than a billion people out of poverty. This achievement—the result of human ingenuity, resilience, and enterprise—gives reason for optimism."[180]

Helms attributes the current progress to the recent expansion of knowledge—the internet allows everyone to know how the world's business is conducted and makes opportunities available to all who want to participate. Helms directs the reader's attention to how the internet has helped the people of Ghana create hundreds of new start-up businesses. "Those startups, and more than 200 others in Ghana, look to the future of the region."[181] If you consider how the widespread use of the printing press 500 years ago helped propel European people to the forefront of the technical-scientific world, just imagine what the internet will do for the people of the world!

**LESSONS FROM THE PAST: MAHATMA GANDHI;
HELPING THE POOREST AND WEAKEST AMONG US**

Mahatma Gandhi found a way to get from India to London as a young man, studied law at the Inner Temple, and was admitted to the bar at age twenty-two in June 1891. After more than twenty years in South Africa, where he used non-violent protests to advance civil rights, he returned to India and worked at organizing peasants, farmers, and urban laborers to protest excessive land-tax and led the movement to gain India's independence from England.

MICRO VS. MACRO ECONOMICS

A TALISMAN

"Whenever you are in doubt, apply the following test. Recall the face of the poorest and weakest man or woman whom you may have seen and ask yourself if the step you contemplate is going to be of any use to him or her.... Will it restore him or her to a control over his or her own life and destiny? Will it lead to swaraj (freedom) for the hungry and spiritually starved millions? Then you will find your doubts and your self melt away."

—MAHATMA GANDHI
(LAST PHASE, VOL. II, 1958, 63)

The haughty officials at the UN could learn a lot from Gandhi's teachings. He told all the people of the world, in his Talisman, that the value of generosity must be measured by how much it helps "the poorest and weakest" among us. Helping those at the bottom is what micro-finance is all about. Why allow the despots of the world to keep doing the opposite—helping themselves while oppressing the hungry and the needy? America has always been the shining city on the hill, the world's best advocate for Liberty, the champion of the poor and downtrodden. Let's live up to that tradition. All we have to do is examine our history, recall how it was done, and help other nations join us in a new world of united and free nations.

SUMMARY

The success that these non-governmental groups have achieved by coaching and financing millions of entrepreneurs shows how simple business activity really is. No experts or consultants needed! No government planning or support needed! Just let them have some property rights, a little coaching, and access to financing and they will do the rest. But if rulers deny those minimal mechanics of good government, they will keep their people in poverty; and most rulers intend to do just that because it leaves more of the country's wealth for the ruling class.

America's foreign policy could be more effective if it placed meaningful emphasis on helping those long-suffering citizens of poorer nations. We first need to agree on how a free economy works, then use that to tame the parasitic elites that subvert fairness. The bottom line: work closely with all nations where freedom is starting to enrich the lives of their people. There is a vacuum to be filled; the people of the poorer nations need our support; and if we do not respond effectively, autocratic nations such as China, Russia and Iran will fill the void for us, extending their power and shoving America aside as an irrelevant actor in world affairs.

In addition, America's obsession with "globalism" needs to be clarified: Global actions, just like "laws and institutions," and "government regulations," can only be judged by whether they directly help the people involved. Mahatma Gandhi told us how it is supposed to work. Read his Talisman and judge our foreign policy accordingly. That would be a simple, humane, and attainable recipe for real progress.

In the next chapter we will look for solutions—how to help the struggling people of the world; how to help everyone hold their heads high and achieve a better fuller life. It would be a mission to make Americans proud. Hint: Don't look to the UN for help.

CHAPTER 15-

Why the UN has Failed to Help the People of the World

 *"Founded in 1945 as a vehicle to avert war and promote human dignity and freedom, the U. N. has instead become a self-serving and ever-expanding haven of privilege for the world's worst regimes, rife with bigotry, fraud, abuse, and corruption, both financial and moral."*
~Claudia Rosett

THE BOTTOM-UP APPROACH OF THE Women's World Bank and Grameen Bank stands in sharp contrast to the failed top-down approach favored by members of the United Nations. The UN is a "deliberative" body as evidenced by its numerous meetings and lengthy reports concerning the world's problems. Missing is any meaningful action to cure those problems. That absence of remedies can be traced to the fact that half the delegates represent totalitarian regimes that have no interest in helping their people. In fact, those regimes want to keep their people poor and oppressed! The result is that the UN does a lot of discussing but accomplishes little.

For example, in 1972, the UN set up a conference to consider the rights of a family to a healthy and productive environment—a subject that, being obvious to a ten-year old, really needs no international conference and meetings! Fast forward 29 years, and in 2012, the United Nations Conference on Sustainable Development (UNCSD), also known as "Rio+20," was held as a twenty-year follow-up to UNCSED. In July 2011, this idea was also picked up by the United Nations Department of Public Information conference in Bonn, Germany. The outcome document proposed seventeen sustainable development goals. At the Rio+20 Conference, a resolution known as "The Future We Want" was reached by member states. Among the key themes agreed on were poverty eradication, energy, water and sanitation, health, and human settlement. (After forty years they were still setting goals!)

A final document was adopted at the UN Sustainable Development Summit on September 25, 2015, when the 193 countries of the UN General Assembly adopted the 2030 Development Agenda titled "Transforming our world: the 2030 Agenda for Sustainable Development." This agenda has ninety-two paragraphs. One paragraph, Paragraph 51, outlines the seventeen Sustainable Development Goals as well as 69 targets and 232 indicators. But it isn't clear how any of it will be accomplished.

Meanwhile, the Grameen Bank and the Women's World Bank have given tens of millions of poor people the opportunity to start their own businesses and allowed them easy access to financing, counseling, and the support of like-minded individuals. The UN's agenda for sustainable development includes little on those critical matters. They have spent the last fifty years just outlining their nice-sounding goals! They seem to have no interest in Gandhi's Talisman. They care little for "the poorest and weakest man or woman." They do not want the step they contemplate "to be of any use to him or her." They do not care about "restoring control over his or her own life and destiny" to such an insignificant person! Instead of helping the weakest and poorest, they have just postured endlessly. Like all the elites of history, those at the UN have just given us smoke and mirrors, hoping to give the illusion that they have good intentions.

The Failure of Mega-Handouts to Autocratic Regimes

The pretense of trying to help the people of poorer nations has also led some people to promote the giving of billions of dollars to those countries, but predictably there has been little to show for it. In *Africa Betrayed*, George B. Ayittey documents how "most of the aid given to the poorest nations has either been stolen or squandered…. It has failed to spur economic growth and has even, in the words of Dr. Rony Brauman, a head of Doctors without Borders, 'unwittingly fueled—and are continuing to fuel—an operation that will be described in hindsight…as one of the greatest slaughters of our time.'"[182]

Authors Klein and Harford have also written about how such past efforts have actually hurt the poorest people by helping their elites maintain control.

> "The ongoing blunder is the direct result of the centrist theories of Western economists and government planners, who believe that only government programs can create prosperity. Their notions are reinforced by ideologues who will go to any lengths to pretend capitalism does not work—and that their social-communal dreams are the wave of the future"[183]

In essence, much of the "aid" has just been the elites of one country giving their people's money to the elites of another country. That's "globalism" gone crazy!

The good news is that in recent years, the world's people have become less isolated, less uninformed: the internet is spreading an awareness of the value of freedom to all people. That is bad news for the elites, because it will become more and more difficult to hold their citizens in ignorance and poverty. Those citizens have seen how much good can come from granting freedom to the smallest members of the economy. Imagine how much more could be accomplished by adding positive support from the major free nations. Imagine a world where our leaders concentrated their efforts on helping the freedom-seeking people of smaller countries instead of making deals with the tyrants that suppress them.

HOW ELITES ARE GOING GLOBAL!

If there is any doubt that the common people of the world are in danger of losing control of their country, the reader need only consider recent meetings of the UN, where members signed onto a "Global Migration Compact." It represents another attempt to pressure all the people of the world to abide by the decrees of globalist elites.

The BBC website reported that leaders in many European nations expressed concern about the UN's action. International law has always maintained that national sovereignty is controlling in matters concerning immigration policies. Hungary's spokesperson said, "This pact poses a threat to the world from the aspect that it could inspire millions [of migrants]." Polish Interior Minister Joachim Brudzinski spoke against the pact, agreeing that it "could also be an incentive for illegal migration."

Speaking before the UN on September 25, 2018, President Trump suggested that "Ultimately, the only long-term solution to the migration crisis is to help people build more hopeful futures in their home countries. Make their countries great again." That suggestion--to fix the problems in countries that make their people want to flee-- would have the potential to both reduce the migration problem and, more importantly, help all the people in such oppressive countries.

The real problem with the UN's position is that while this one will be largely ignored, the push to gain authority over its member states is gaining strength. In New Zealand, officials had two major reservations: The compact fails to distinguish between legal and illegal immigration, and that signing up to such agreements obliges the country to put in place the principles and follow the policies dictated by the UN. Failure to follow through on any of them would create pressure on a signor to adjust their policies to conform or expose them to the risk that their own courts will hold them to the standard committed to. And one of the UN's required "standards" is to monitor and prosecute discriminatory speech or writing that denigrates immigrants. Only a lawyer can like such litigious and profitable possibilities that would emanate from signing onto such a vague and undefined liability.

Sadly, many Americans will approve of such mandates, either because it will enhance their careers and wealth or because they will get to feel good for supporting such "kind" intentions.

But one-half of the 195 member nations send delegates to the UN who represent the elites of their dictatorial regimes, and those regimes have little interest in being kind. They *want* their disgruntled citizens to leave!

IS THE UN JUST THE LEAGUE OF NATIONS ALL OVER AGAIN?

In a refreshing essay, Claudia Rosett has explained why the U.N.'s basic design means it cannot be reformed and why we must seek alternatives:

> "It's time to break the taboo, and to bring fully into America's foreign policy debates, the question of how to dispense with the U.N. altogether."[184]

The fundamental problem with the United Nations is that approximately one-half the members do not subscribe to the UN's stated mandate to help the people of the world. And we give them money! It would be more fruitful to concentrate our attention on the other half of the nations: those that attempt to honor human rights and grant freedom for their people.

America has wasted trillions of dollars, and sacrificed many lives, especially in the Middle East, using military might to impose its own values on others. Such efforts have proven to be disasters for all concerned. However, there are many countries gradually moving toward freedom where our support could help and would be appreciated by most of their people. More than one-half of the 180 nations measured in the Heritage Index of Freedom are considered "mostly free" or better. If we want to advance freedom throughout the world our foreign policy should be directed at encouraging those nations, even rewarding them, for each advance their people enjoy. Unfortunately, our elites ignore those nations, and prefer to attend international conferences and gain photo opportunities signing meaningless treaties with despotic rulers.

There are more and more nations where the internet has informed the people of the exciting possibilities that come from free economies. Our foreign policies should be directed at encouraging and helping those people gain the rights and laws that allow them unrestricted access to their economies. Americans should consider that approach or otherwise we will just continue doing what hasn't worked for the last seventy-five years. And that is akin to insanity!

THE UN'S RECORD OF FAILED FOREIGN AID

The truth is that past "aid" programs have poured trillions of dollars into the poor nations of the world for over seventy-five years with little benefit for their people. The government officials in charge did not ensure that enabling institutions were present—the very same infrastructure of laws and financial supports that all the historians and economists write about as needed for successful societies.

There have been a few economists who have pointed out how wasteful these expensive efforts have proven. Such scholars as Hernando de Soto, Julian Simon, and P. T. Bauer have documented the folly of past assistance practices, and their books have been published by distinguished publishers. But they have been neglected by the academics, media, and experts who do not like the solutions they offer. For example, Bauer suggests that "foreign aid...was not indispensable for the progress of poor countries, and that it often served to underwrite and prolong extremely damaging policies pursued in the name of comprehensive planning."[185]

Bauer also indicated that many of the charitable organizations that have engaged in the lucrative business of collecting gifts from well-meaning individuals were more interested in expanding their operation and salaries than making sure the funds were used effectively. Bauer writes, "There is much truth in Professor Thomas Sowell's observation that the poor are a gold mine."[186]

Bauer also has pointed out that there were many nations such as Singapore, Chile, South Korea, and the Arab Emirates where, during the post-WWII years, considerable economic progress has been made without outside aid. Such progress, he writes, "was not the result...of the forced mobilization of their resources...or governmental central planning...or the adoption by governments of economic development as a formal policy goal. What happened was in large measure the result of the individual voluntary responses of millions of people to emerging or expanding opportunities... These developments were made possible by firm but limited government, without large expenditures of public funds and without the receipt of large external subventions."[187]

Bauer thereby confirms the lesson of history as detailed in this book: progress for the common people of a nation comes from a limited government and an open economy which allows the voluntary responses of millions of people. Sadly, opposition to such a realistic solution is to be expected because most consultants, academics, and experts favor having economies directed by elites at the top. They adore "comprehensive planning"—it's what they do; it's the only thing they can do! Because the academics and major media are increasingly allied with the elites, it is their message that keeps being repeated for public consumption and in the classrooms of America.

Hernando De Soto, the noted Peruvian economist, made the problem clear and simple in his book *The Mystery of Capitalism*. His colleagues documented how something as simple as a Registry of Deeds, and laws protecting private property, are notoriously deficient in most third world nations. He also clearly presents the arithmetic showing that the richest nations on earth could give the poorer nations seven-tenths of a percent of their GDP every year for seventy years and the amounts transferred would not equal what the poor citizens of those nations already possess.[188]

The glitch is that those citizens do not fully "possess" their assets. Because their laws governing land ownership are so faulty, without a proper Registry of Deeds, most of the people have had to just claim an empty piece of land and build a shanty there to house their families. They are squatters and have no rights to the property. Result: They cannot sell or mortgage their homes. They are locked in a frozen economy. Their assets are rendered worthless because their elites have blocked the institutions that provide security of ownership.

Instead of us giving their elites money, it would make more sense to encourage the people of a poor country to establish deed registries, banks to provide mortgages, and laws to protect private property. That has not happened for two reasons: 1) Our elites prefer to be involved in handing out taxpayer money, and 2) Most of the delegates to the UN prefer to keep their people in bondage and get rich countries to just give them money. That is why the fundamental problems in poor nations have not been rectified: simply because their elites oppose any reforms that might reduce their own personal advantages and our elites want the power that dispensing money gives them.

HOW SIMPLE COMMON SENSE SOLVES MOST PROBLEMS

If we accept the obvious fact that almost all progress (or stagnation) in every nation's condition is caused by its people, we do not even need economic theorists. What De Soto and Bauer have told us, that has been suppressed by the elites, is really just simple common sense:

1. If free people make things happen, will an economy be helped by restricting their peoples' efforts? No, it is self-evident that the people should not be shackled.

2. If some people seek to gain unfair advantage over others, should such efforts be regulated? Yes, it is self-evident that

anyone seeking special advantages for themselves must be regulated, blocked, and, if necessary, prosecuted.

3. Should the economy be open to all on equal terms? Yes, just as in a sports event, the competition must be fair and open to all. (Would you really want the NBA to require that players for the Hornets carry 50-pound backpacks, play barefoot, and follow the rules, while those from the Knicks would get Air-Jordan sneakers and could cheat however they wish? Such obviously unfair rules are what the common people of the world are being subjected to!

4. What is the role of those in government? Obviously, they are there to manage the essential government functions, honestly and efficiently, maintain a just legal system, protect the people from foreign interference, and maintain the integrity and fairness of all institutions and political/economic activities.

Whoever seeks to undermine those foundational principles—the principles of fairness, liberty, justice, and equal rights, is an enemy of the common people. In 1775, it was the king and his aristocrats, and we threw them out. Today, it is the elites in every nation who seek to gain special advantages over their people, and it is from them that we must now *take back* the rights to freedom and equal treatment.

CAN "FREEDOM" BE MEASURED?

For the last few decades, the relative degree of economic freedom and human rights enjoyed by the people in almost 200 nations has been ranked each year by several non-governmental organizations. When the 186 countries scored for economic freedom in 2017 are divided into four quartiles, countries in the top quartile averaged $43,342 per capita income, the second quartile is less than half at $20,255, the third at less than half the second at $8,384, and the bottom quartile has a lowly average per capita income of $7,217. The correlation between economic freedom and per capita income is overwhelming.[189]

HERITAGE FOUNDATION

RANKINGS OF SELECTED ECONOMIES

2017 INDEX OF ECONOMIC FREEDOM

1-Hong Kong 89.8	17-United States 75.1
2-Singapore 88.6	18-Denmark 75.12
3-New Zealand 83.7	25-Norway 74.0
4-Switzerland 81.5	26-Germany 73.8
5-Australia 81.0	36-Israel 69.7
6-Estonia 79.1	40-Japan 69.6
7-Canada 78.5	45-Poland 68.3
8-United A. E. 76.9	69-Spain 63.6
9-Ireland 76.7	72-France 63.3
10-Chile 76.5	111-China 57.4
11-Taiwan 76.5	114-Russia 57.3
12-U.K. 76.4	143-India 52.6
13-Georgia 76.0	178-Cuba 33.9
14-Luxembourg 75.9	179-Venezuela 27.0
15-Netherlands 75.8	189-No. Korea 4.9

The top five nations, with scores over 80, are labeled "free." Those nations scoring between 70 and 80, twenty-nine in all, are labeled "mostly free." Ninety-two nations are labeled "moderately free." Almost half the nations, eighty-eight in all, scored below 60, with sixty-five called "mostly unfree," and the twenty-three scoring below 50 are considered "repressed. It is sad to see America ranked at #17, below such nations as Estonia, Ireland, Chile, and Taiwan.

These rankings explain why the Grameen Bank has even set up offices in some of America's major inner cities. Those American citizens apparently need the same help as the poorest in Africa. Shame on American schools! Shame on those city's politicians!

The dozens of economists who determine these annual rankings represent a large number of nations and are in full agreement over the criteria used: the respect for human rights, the ease of doing business, judicial effectiveness, government integrity, a low tax burden, and the extent of enabling institutions that facilitate free business and financial transactions.

Thus, the criteria used to measure each nation are clearly defined and, more importantly, the direct link between freedom and prosperity is now documented. However, the elites still manage to block the reforms needed to create prosperity and liberty for their people. And the media make no effort to publicize such suppression.

SUMMARY

Any country can spread the level of prosperity more widely among its people by simply adopting the well-established policies that work. It's not theory; it is a "truth" demonstrated by the record of history for thousands of years. However, almost all elites are determined to thwart every attempt to allow equal opportunity or true freedom for their oppressed people. They just want to get more, the lion's share. And they see nothing wrong with that desire or whatever devious means are required to satisfy their greed.

Recent autocratic rulers in China have tried to mimic Western capitalism by encouraging private businesses while still retaining despotic control of their people. Their elites want to have their cake and eat it too! It remains to be seen how long their people will put up with this tyranny. We do know that leaders in Iran, Russia, Germany, and Japan have in the past, at least briefly, appeared successful with such a hybrid system. However, that success was not long-lived. There is no substitute for personal liberty and sooner or later it finds a way to burst out.

The people of all free nations must demand that their government's international efforts be aimed at working with nations based strictly on their progress in providing opportunities for their people. Instead of giving billions of dollars to oppressive nations, we should be penalizing them until they put in place the reforms needed to help their people. Any logical part of a solution should also be to dissolve the United Nations, close the offices, disconnect the phones and computers, and send all the haughty and corrupt members home where they came from.

The spacious UN headquarters on the East River, or any comparable facilities in America, could then be recycled to house a new "United Free Nations" (UFN), which would be made up exclusively of "qualified" members. Membership would be determined by how a nation scored on such Indices as the Fraser or Heritage Index of Economic Freedom and the Human Rights Watch World Report. Possibly, that would provide an incentive for borderline nations to try and qualify. It would also make clear to the people of oppressed nations that we are on their side and there is a clear and simple alternative to their suffering.

The role of such leadership was illustrated more than fifty years ago by JFK in his speech to the oppressed East German people when he told them that he "was also a Berliner" and that he understood their suffering. President Ronald Reagan did him one better, about 35 years later, when he stood in Berlin and told the Soviet Premier to "take down this wall!" Now is the time to return to such proactive and compassionate ways. What has gone wrong in American governance since those days? Instead of speaking out like presidents Kennedy and Reagan, instead of standing for freedom, some of our leaders are meeting with foreign dictators and making lucrative personal financial deals for themselves and their families!

During the Cold War, America sponsored *Radio Free Europe* to inform all citizens living under oppressive elites that there is a better way and a better future. Our foreign policy must restate that message of hope rather than going around bombing and assassinating supposed enemies. Now is the time for Americans to work with other nations to make the reforms needed so they too can boast of having a government OF the people, FOR the people, and BY the people. That would be a "globalist" strategy that we could all be proud of

Such a humanitarian policy could be the most effective defense against the ongoing effort by China, Iran, and Russia to gain dominance around the world. The way to defeat autocratic bullies is to make it clear to their suffering citizens that there is a better way, that they can

join the forces of freedom, and all they have to do is fight for justice and a fair economy. America and its free allies would then be standing on the right side of history, helping all people of the world achieve a better destiny.

CHAPTER 16-

Where Do We Go from Here?

*The conservative more-or-less half of American
life is living under an alien regime that means to
continue harming us socially and morally just
as much as economically. Plainly, we find ourselves in a…
state of war. The beginning of such safety as we may work out for
ourselves is to regard our rulers as they regard us.*
by Angelo M. Codevilla, November 20, 2020
Article on American Greatness

THE FACTIONS CURRENTLY DIVIDING AMERICA may be
described simply as 1) those who favor a large and controlling government, and 2) those who emphasize personal freedom and a limited government. The two groups have become so hardened in their
positions that our future as a united country is threatened. However,
this breakdown of our political system is primarily due to a small third
faction: the elite who stir the pot, encourage a big nanny government,
and deliberately create division--just to maintain their political control.

A weakness of democracies is that they depend on a moral and
honorable citizenry, self-reliant, independent, and devoted to building
a unified community. Such people understand what Ronald Reagan

meant when he told us that "Government cannot solve our problems; government is the problem!" Unfortunately, elites gradually seduce even strong-willed individuals with an appeal that Marina Medvin describes as "that of a man in a van luring unsuspecting kids inside with promises of candy and puppies."

That is also why President Obama was only half-right when he told us that "You didn't earn it; the government did it for you." His first four words were certainly correct in pointing out that we, the last couple generation, did not earn the richness and liberty we enjoy in today's democracies. That rich endowment was bequeathed to us by earlier generations. But he was quite wrong in his last six words—how the government gave us the bounty of this nation—the truth is that we had little or no government for the first 300 years when prior generations of Americans built the country to world supremacy.

Our current generation is, in fact, much like the third generation of a once wealthy family, consuming their inherited fortunes, forgetting good habits, and liquidating what their forefathers bequeathed them. Claiming that the government created America is the way elites are attempting to erase our past, all so they can fill the void as our saviors!

Our elites pursue their selfish objective by denigrating families, religion, thrift, self-reliance, moral behavior, and condemning our parents and grandparents as racist, evil, greedy, and immoral. They have employed what George Orwell called "Double Think" in order to label those who built the nation as bad, and the current generation that is living off that legacy as victims. That argument is patently ludicrous if you think about if for a minute: Because the last few generations have been born into the freest and richest country on earth, how can those who built it be damned?

There are still improvements to be made, yes, but no other people have ever done it as well. Rather than dismantling this success story we should be working to help the people of other nations gain the freedom and affluence we enjoy. Of course, our leaders will fight such a policy because they identify more with other elites than with the ordinary people of the world. Elites simply consider us to be deplorable, beneath them, and not deserving of equal authority.

That's where our elites are coming from. There is a method in that madness: The elites need to destroy our strengths, our past, and our independence so they can rule untroubled by the resistance of free people. And they also have no interest in helping all the other common people of the world.

RE-ESTABLISHING TRUTH AND REASON

Partisan debate has become inflamed by ideological battles that the elites foment simply to divide the voters and gain personal power. That elite is supported by the leaders of both political parties, and they have all continued to defraud the public while debating partisan flash points. However, buried in all their BS, there can be gleaned some important policy differences.

In Matthew Continetti's words, when the USSR crumbled, the obvious failure of managed economies, controlled by bureaucrats, "presented a challenge for the Left: how to carry on the fight against capitalism when its major ideological alternative was no longer viable... [so] instead of presenting collectivism and central planning as the ideal form of government, Marx's class struggle was reformulated into an ethno-racial struggle—a ceaseless competition between colonizer and colonized, victimizer and victim, oppressor and oppressed."[190]

Academics joined the fray, revising their courses to emphasize the evils in America's past: the atomic bombs dropped on Japan, the cruelty of slavery, segregation, racial and religious bigotry, the oppression of women, the horrors of European colonialism, our subjugation of Native Americans, etc. Many students may have recognized the weakness of Russian communism, but they were taught to also have little respect for their country, its history, or their family heritage.

One way that the elite have denigrated America has been to advance the idea that many other countries are equal to, or superior to America. Thus, "multiculturalism" has become the liberals' mantra. But think it over: Isn't it extraordinarily illogical to praise all cultures as equal and admirable while denouncing America's?

The elite's game plan is to treat minority groups as victims of systemic racism and intolerance imposed on them by an oppressive white majority and its racist and unjust capitalistic culture. However, the truth is that it is the elites who are the oppressors and the victimizers, while *all* the common people are the oppressed and the victims.

Why not set aside ideologies, regulate the marketplace so there is no favoritism, rationalize the thousands of welfare programs, and prosecute corruption and conflicts of interest ruthlessly? Makes sense, but the elites will never agree—they love favoritism, loopholes, and corruption.

PERHAPS A NEW ACTION PLAN IS NEEDED?

Continetti ended a talk at Hillsdale College with the optimistic suggestion that "the mystic chords of memory...will yet swell the chorus of the Union, when again touched, as surely they will be, by the better angels of our nature." That is a stirring hope but, unfortunately, there is nothing angelic about America's resident enemies; they are determined to destroy our valuable traditions, vilify our unique history, and undermine our culture of self-reliance and individual liberty.

James Burnham, in *Suicide of the West*, detailed this same story half a century ago, how the ideas of the liberal Left "work like a spiritual worm, corrupting the will of the West to survive as a distinctive historical entity..."[191] Unfortunately, such astute observations, issued repeatedly for over half a century, have not altered our downward trajectory. James Burnham is an ignored footnote in history, just as those spinning the same argument today will probably be forgotten tomorrow.

The question is whether the American people will act in unison and set things straight. In his book about "the ruling class," Angelo Codevilla points out the difficulty of restoring our strength and culture, but he suggests that the revolution the ruling class is pursuing to transform America will prove unsustainable. "They may win some elections by arguing that its opponents are stupid, etc.... But America's majority long since withdrew its confidence from a class that has earned, and has no way of shedding, the image of pretentious, incompetent losers."[192]

However, author Codevilla may be overly optimistic: more and more people are siding with those pretentious elites. They have the schools and media trumpeting their righteousness. Their revolution to transform America appears to be ongoing and quite sustainable. And the majority of voters who oppose those policies have been divided into two opposing camps by the elites.

Unless a responsible leadership emerges that can unite a majority, get them to vote, then count the vote properly, and remove those pretentious losers from power, we will become, as Burnham writes, "the willing assistants to our own suicide." And if the elites win enough elections, and keep corrupting the voting process, they will, sooner or later, adjust the laws so that even our power to resist will be removed.

Perhaps we should face the fact that theoretical arguments about economics, calls for a return to patriotism and pride in our country, and entreaties for all to work in harmony for the good of America, no matter how brilliantly they are composed and presented, will not stop the fatal course we are taking. Indeed, the scholarly members of

America's leading conservative publications and think tanks may be the last to accept the fact that it appears very possible, if not probable, that all the current learned debates between conservatives and liberals will have zero effect on America's future.

One-half of today's voters care little for such arguments, even as profound as they most certainly are; nor do they care a whit about past proven results that could provide a guide for future policy. They have never been taught history! And, more than half are just not interested! Perhaps after a half century of we the people losing the battle, fifty long years of gradual retreat, a change of tactics is in order?

The inescapable fact is that those people seeking to undermine and transform America are winning! They have been winning for more than half a century! Their attacks on America's heart and soul have grown stronger and the opposition has done no more than slow it down. It is ironic that those who oppose big government and point out all the failings of socialism are, in their own way, just as harmful as their opponents. Many of the conservatives on the "Right" side of the debate do little to clean up the capitalist system that the Left attacks. The favored treatment of big business, the unfair tax code, the subsidies and pork doled out to the wealthy, and hundreds of regulations that minimize competition have combined to corrupt the free market.

CONTROLLING OUR LEADERS

"We cannot achieve equality without first achieving some measure of accountability for those at the top."

~~ CHRISTOPHER HAYES

TWILIGHT OF THE ELITES, 235

Bernie Sanders is right to criticize what has become a mercantilist, or crony, capitalism. Indeed, many of Bernie's supporters are in agreement with the base that is attracted to President Trump. Both those camps are filled with the same types of voters--the ignored and suppressed American workers. The elites have marginalized all those people, made them work harder and longer, while sucking off more and more of the nation's bounty for themselves.

In brief, our leaders on both the Right and the Left have justified Bernie's attacks as well as those from Trump's base. For example, the 2009 bailout of the corrupt financial institutions was a bi-partisan effort. Can you believe it? The one thing both political parties agreed on was the need to quickly bail out Wall Street! The bankers, with help from the media, sold the public that line about "Banks too Big to Fail." They did it by using the same techniques as Kraft uses to sell ketchup. The "Father of Advertising," Edward Bernays, has pointed out that the common people never know the "invisible" forces that spread false knowledge and propaganda by shaping the thoughts and values of the masses.

Just as Bernays predicted, many voters believed that the country's entire financial structure could be destroyed unless the government came to the rescue. Then, in 2008, George Bush and Barack Obama worked together like a well-oiled machine, spent a trillion dollars, quickly, to rescue the bankers who had brought on the massive financial melt-down. And no one went to jail! No wonder the average voter tuned out.

The good news is that the corrupt practices of the elite have become so egregious that voters from the Right and the Left may unite to vent their frustration. Members of the middle class and upper middle class now share what Christopher Hayes describes as "a sense of betrayal, injustice, and dissolution... a sense that they are no longer in control, that some small corrupt core of elites can launch an idiotic war, or bail out the banks, or mandate health insurance, and despite their relative privilege and education and money and social capital there's not a damn thing they can do about it."[193]

Past democracies have never proven safe from the great sweeping forces that have almost invariably led to their demise. The persistent drive by elites to gain power over the people eventually wears down all opposition. The people in mature democracies eventually become apathetic and dependent, willing to trade their liberty for security. That loss of vigilance is what allows the ever-waiting elites to subvert the laws, grab control of the government, and proclaim a clear final signal of the nation's inevitable decline.

THE VALUE OF LEADERSHIP

"We shall fight on the beaches, we shall fight on the landing grounds, we shall fight in the fields and in the streets, we shall fight in the hills; we shall never surrender."

~ WINSTON CHURCHILL, APRIL 6, 1940

Let us pray that there are still enough true Americans, individuals who cherish their liberty, reject the promises of government aid, and determined enough to reverse the historic tides eroding our nation's foundation. The challenge before us, finding a way for a huge and heterogeneous nation to unite and maintain its democratic and energetic nature, may prove to be insolvable. Note that when Churchill rallied his people to resist Nazism, he was inspiring them "to fight on the beaches," to resist a foreign enemy; today, we must fight a different enemy, fellow Americans, who are already entrenched in our midst.

Any honest observer would have to agree that our national destiny seems to be inexorably tracing the path of prior great nations, burdened by democracy's two natural enemies: a rapidly growing, heterogeneous, and divided population, and the burden of an expanding Leviathan bureaucracy that is smothering our freedom. And, to make matters worse, in the past century, we have seen a new third enemy emerge: the rise of an abstract thinking elite, a divisive force that has gained control of academia and the media, working to further the coercive power of government, while tearing down our statues and leaving our unity, our flag, and patriotism in tatters.

If Professor Tytler could see us today, he might suggest that, with this added internal foe, our national destiny might come full circle even faster than the eclipses of prior free nations. Just as even an enterprising and resilient people cannot fully succeed economically without the safety and support of empowering legal and financial institutions, so a nation, even one replete with such supports, cannot succeed if its people are burdened by a corrupt elite, visionary but misguided dreamers, and the swelling ranks of a discouraged class that looks for ever-greater assistance from the government.

The task before us is monumental; no half measures will restore the pride, unity, and initiative of our people. If the Republic is to be saved, such a happier future outcome can only be gained by extreme disruptive action. Debating theories, finetuning our immigration laws, and limiting abortions will not reverse the current Decline. Such a disruptive plan could only be led by a strong leader possessing a clear vision and the determination, conviction, and skills to get things done!

Trump's victory at the polls in 2016, upsetting both Republican and Democratic establishments, may be a sign that enough voters remain who understand the need for plain talk, common sense, and ACTION. Indeed, a major reason to vote for candidates like Elizabeth Warren and Donald Trump is that the elites are all united to destroy them! With enemies like that, they must be good!

The current problem is twofold: First, political debate has become focused between the Right and the Left and argued so viciously that many voters opt for a middle-of-the-road course, thinking that the middle ground provides a reasoned compromise between the two alternate courses. But, if the Right seeks to maintain a free economy and limit government powers, and the Left wants to totally transform America, the middle ground is one constantly moving to the Left, albeit slowly, but still continuously to our detriment and to the advantage of the ruling elite. The result to date has been an ever-larger bureaucracy regulating our businesses, our personal lives, our schools, and recently, our elections.

The other problem is that intellectuals, both the conservative and liberal deep thinkers, are much too cranial! They quibble over who is a true liberal, the exact meaning of words like "progressive," and offer bland calls to restore the Founders' principles to guide us forward—as if such vague intellectual concepts resonate with any significant number of voters.

Instead of debating abstractions and personalities, it is essential to direct our efforts to specific policies that will restore true capitalism, free of loopholes, restrictions, and subsidies. Unless the basic economic system is returned to operate as a fair marketplace, open to all, the voters will gradually flee to the big government camp for help and the elites will win. As long as the public sees inequities in the basic system, the appeal of socialist remedies will gain more adherents.

The elites know all this: by making the government more and more corrupt, and the economy more and more unfair, the elites gain more and more voters who will support their cynical promises to fix things.

However, restoring a fair economic system will not be enough. We must restructure the educational system, make the curriculum useful to the average student, tame the elites, reform entitlements, restore states' rights, and substantially reduce foreign entanglements. I doubt many of the writers, talking heads, or politicians would fully endorse any of those policies. Instead, they would point out the pros and cons, suggest limits on the extent of any action, and warn about every conceivable negative consequence that might arise from anyone actually doing anything. Such wobbly hesitancy, from inexperienced thinkers, will not save America. In fact, getting the people muddled with complicated argumentation benefits the elites, helps them divide the people, and thereby paves the way for them to gain added control over our lives.

DO WE HAVE TIME TO REVERSE THE DOWNWARD SPIRAL?

There may be a window of opportunity; the good news is that the life cycles of democracies rise and fall slowly; it will probably be only our great-grandchildren, or even theirs, who would be seriously affected by the apparent gradual but continuing collapse of America.

The solution would be for the common people, including their intellectual advocates, to join forces, get beyond the fine distinctions that distract them from the primary goals, and take decisive action. The blatant power of big government and multi-billionaires needs to be neutered. Currently, the elites are allied with one objective: to help themselves at our expense and they appear to be an "irresistible force." Without a persistent and "unmovable counter-force," such as us, those advocates of a huge all-controlling state will win.

THE PROBLEM WITH GOVERNMENT

"History makes it plain that unless restrained, government proliferates to a point where it bankrupts the people at the same time it robs them of their freedom."

~~ RONALD REAGAN

We must think in a new way. The accompanying text box shows how President Reagan, using only 27 words, summed up this problem. It is not complicated, nor is it just one more theory. We know that big government destroys freedom and promotes corruption. We know that corrupt leaders lust after the power that big government bestows on them. We know that an open and fair free market creates the most prosperity for all. We know that elites and greedy capitalists have always tried to corrupt the free market to gain personal advantage. We know that the lure of socialism is to overcome the unfairness to the common people that comes from corrupt elites and greedy individuals. Therefore, we know that the solution is to maintain a fair free market with minimal government by taming the elites. That is where we can look to sports, Joe Kennedy, and the newspapers for guidance:

1. In sports, there are rules and honest and experienced referees who penalize cheating. But, in governmental matters, we have let the partisan divide overcome the application of justice. If a member of "our" side cheats many of us will ignore it. Prosecution of corruption has to be impartial, intensive, and voters have to help. Presently voters routinely re-elect known cheaters, the kind of people they wouldn't want to play sports or bridge with.

2. Joe Kennedy helped President Roosevelt (FDR) rein in the speculative cheats on Wall Street after the devastating financial crash of 1929. Kennedy knew how to do that, from personal experience, and his rules worked for over sixty years until they were removed in the 1990s. Removing restraints on themselves is what corrupt elites do, but few noticed when the controls on Wall Street under Glass-Steagall were eliminated and corrupt financiers took advantage. Joe Kennedy's reforms were cancelled by the elites and that "win" restored their license to steal.

3. The media has failed America. Instead of helping the public keep an eye on the governing class, it has joined the elites. The major media is owned by big corporate interests, and instead of protecting the public, it promotes the powerful interests that seek to gain the country's riches and control its destiny. All we can do is boycott their message. We need some good old-fashioned muckrakers because there is a lot of muck in the swamps.

Perhaps the underlying and more fundamental problem is that Americans have lost their moral compass. A democracy can only work with a moral people. But even if you set aside morals and religion altogether, you should still have to follow the rules. Think of a baseball game or a football game that is played with no rules! It would be chaos! The same principle applies to a free marketplace—it can only work with observance of the rules, and the rules should all be aimed at one thing—providing opportunity for all to participate with equal justice applied and enforced. Otherwise, the elites will keep us going back to a mercantilist or corrupt capitalism, where the cheats win, win, win.

If we do not find a way to restore the free economy and control the greedy elites, it will just be a matter of time before America completes its passage around Tytler's circle, following the Fatal Sequence that the wise Scot discovered and outlined so clearly for all to see. Let us prevent that from happening; let's take our nation back from those who would destroy it!

WAYS TO SAVE AMERICA: VIGILANCE, VOTE, OR VENUS

The history of free nations tells us that there are three ways to keep the good times rolling. One of those, a total and bloody revolution, which has worked in the past, is probably not possible today. The armed militias of the past, featuring common folk, armed with pitchforks and muskets, had a chance to win that may never exist again. That leaves two ways to preserve our freedom: Stay Vigilant and Vote!

Vigilance by the people of a nation must be maintained or elites will change the rules, tamper with the laws, and gain an unyielding grip on everyone's destiny. Americans have already allowed too many changes that empower the elites, increase the inequalities of wealth, and over-regulate the activity of enterprising people. In Chapter twelve we described how the Venetians kept a close watch on their elites for 900 years, constantly ready to depose any who were doing more harm than good. And we saw that after 900 years they were not paying attention and the elites in a very short period changed enough institutions so that they gained firm control. That was when Venice began its decline from a great civilization to a tourist destination.

The lesson to be gained is that we must take a little time away from the Super Bowl, the game shows, the Hollywood gossip, and even fishing and hunting, so we can check on our elites. They are not beyond our control—we can keep the nation working right only if we are ever vigilant and on guard.

Vote in every election and find the common-sense candidate who will help take our country back, who will not toady up to the establishment, who will fight for Mahatma Gandhi's Talisman, and who will stay true to our founding moral principles.

Also, voters must focus on what's fundamentally at stake. Don't put too much emphasis on the many social issues that will not seriously determine the fortune of the nation over the next fifty years—like gun control, abortion rights, gender issues, climate control, removing historic statues, and punishing politically incorrect speech. In place of such issues, look for candidates of unquestioned integrity, demonstrated experience and wisdom, a passion for an economy open equally to all participants, and an implacable opposition to favoring special interests or tolerating unequal application of the laws. With those kinds of people running the government, the other issues would be well tended to. But if we keep electing zealots and crooks, nothing will be done right.

IS THERE A NEW PLACE TO SETTLE IF ALL ELSE FAILS?

If the world's population continues past growth rates, our farmers and technocrats will probably be able to feed everyone, but how will we all manage to co-exist, find employment, and cooperate in huge social settings, with people massed into tighter and tighter quarters? It will not be a happy or pastoral setting, and constant ideological battles, distorted news, riots, and violent partisan protests will not make it any more pleasant.

It is possible that the few remaining expanses of undeveloped land may provide a new "start-up" community for those adventurous enough to find it and inhabit it, but such new places will eventually become impossible to find. Science fiction, however, does provide a possible solution. Space exploration suggests that we will find habitable planets somewhere in the universe and our small cadre of space travelers might be able to search them out and settle there. (As a by-product, such taming of hostile environments, with humans making comfortable abodes for themselves in space, should end all the ridiculous arguments that advantageous geography, climate, and riverways caused the progress of Homo sapiens. People have overcome every such obstacle to success—except for the physical and mental oppression of domineering elites!)

History has shown that start-up nations do well. Our astronauts are a special breed; they could very well set a new all-time record for building a great new nation, even faster and better than the American settlers did 400 years ago. And it may come to be the only solution available because the world's elites are determined to undo everything that helps the common people or limits their own insatiable greed.

Luckily, a new "start-up" nation in space may not be necessary, for the good news is that exciting new possibilities of freedom are currently being realized in many areas of the world. Sure, the elites are winning in the "mature" Western democracies, and holding fast in the numerous despotic nations, but there are places where the elites are losing! Losing to freedom! Losing even to the relatively unsophisticated people of such "less developed" places as Ghana, Indonesia, Uganda, and Chile. Obviously, anyone can do it if they set the elites aside! The human race is extraordinary and everyone, in every nation, is proving to possess the same great abilities, just waiting for the freedom to unleash their untapped potential and apply their common genius.

Maybe we can make it work right here on earth. Why give up without a fight? Why not spread the message of freedom to all the people living in poorer nations? Building a new free nation in space wouldn't be easy! And we have America here, now, in our grasp. Why not just save America, restore our supportive communities, end the ideological bickering, and save our descendants from the need to go to some wilderness in space to start anew? Doesn't it make more sense to just be vigilant, vote, and tame the elites destroying our country?

ENDNOTES

1 Simon Sinek, Leaders Eat Last: Why Some Teams Pull Together and Others Don't (New York: Portfolio/Penguin,
2017), 81-86 & cover jacket.

2 Ibid., 80, 86

3 From an article posted at SayWhyDoI.com by Lior (on
February 22, 2011).

4 Yuval Noah Harari, Sapiens: A Brief History of Humankind
(New York: Harper Perennial, 2018), 4

5 Colin Renfrew, Prehistory, The Making of the Modern
Mind (New York: The Modern Library, 2008), 92

6 Harari, op. cit., 4

7 Ibid., 9

8 Colin Renfrew, op. cit., 79

9 Harari, op. cit., 16

10 Ibid., 8, 18

11 Ibid., 21

12 Ibid., 32

13 Merlin Donald, Origin of the Human Mind: Three Stages
in the Evolution of Culture and Cognition (Cambridge,
MA: Harvard University Press, 1991), 382

14 Harari, op. cit., 88

15 Douglas Preston, The Lost City of the Monkey Gods (New
York: Grand Central Publishing, 2017), 79

16 Harari, op. cit., 86

17 Acemoglu & Robinson, Why Nations Fail: The Origins of
Power, Prosperity, and Poverty, 2012 (New York: Curren-
cy- Crown Publishing Group, 2012), 139

18 Harari, op. cit., 79

19 Ibid., 72

20 Ibid., 74

21 Lee Habeeb, The Story of the Gettysburg Address, Newsweek.com, November 19, 2020

22 Ibid.

23 Douglas Preston, op. cit., 208–209

24 Ibid., 209

25 G. William Domhoff, Who Rules America: The Triumph of the Corporate Rich (New York McGraw-Hill Educational, 2014)

26 Ibid, 220

27 Scott Armstrong, The Seersucker Theory: The Value of Experts in Forecasting (Technology Review, June, 1980)

28 Dan Gardner, Future Babble: Why Pundits are Hedgehogs and Foxes Know Best (New York: Plume Books, Penguin Group, 2011), 15

29 Angelo M. Codevilla, The Ruling Class: How They Corrupted America and What We Can Do About It (New York: Beaufort Books, 2010), xix

30 Jeffrey A. Winters, Oligarchy (New York: Cambridge University Press, 2011), 211

31 Ibid., 285

32 Ibid., 285

33 Ibid., 285

34 Bill Greene, Saving Democracy: How Good Management Could Trump Ideological Bickering (North Charleston, SC: Create Space Independent Publishing, 2016), 237–8

35 Tucker Carlson, Ship of Fools: How a Selfish Ruling Class Is Bringing America to the Brink of Revolution (New

York: Free Press, 2018), 14

36 Codevilla, op. cit., xix

37 Jean-Francois Revel, Anti-Americanism (San Francisco: Encounter Books, 2000), 13

38 Victor Davis Hanson, The Other Greeks: The Family Farm and the Agrarian Roots of Western Civilization (Berkeley, CA: University of California Press, 1999) xiv

39 Ibid., xiv

40 Ibid., xvi

41 Jean-Francois Revel, op. cit., 13

42 Hanson, op. cit., 4

43 R. J. Hopper, The Early Greeks (New York: Harper & Row Publishers, 1976), 107

44 Ibid., 104

45 William H. McNeill, The Rise of the West: A History of the Human Community (Chicago: Chicago University Press, 1991), 264

46 Acemoglu & Robinson, op. cit., 159

47 Ibid, 163

48 Ibid., 164

49 Ibid., 168

50 Christopher Hibbert, Venice: The Beginning of a City (New York: W. W. Norton, 1989), 5

51 John Ruskin, The Stones of Venice (Mount Kisco, NY: Moyer Bell Limited, 1989), 12

52 Mancur Olson, Power and Prosperity (New York; Basic Books, 2000), 39-40

53 Machiavelli, The Prince and Other Writings (New York: Barnes & Noble Classic, 2003), xxvii

54 The Heritage Society, The Annual Index of Economic

Freedom. The last two chapters of this book will develop the significance of the spreading adoption of open economies around the world.

55 Gregory Clark, A Farewell to Alms: A Brief History of Economic World History (Princeton NJ: Princeton University Press, 2008), 373

56 Acemoglu & Robinson, op. cit., 159

57 Ludwig Von Mises, Human Action: A Treatise on Economics, 4th Rev. Ed. (Irvington-On-Hudson NY: The Foundation for Economic Education, Inc. 1996), 8

58 Johan Norberg, Progress: Ten Reasons to Look Forward to the Future (London UK, 2017)

59 Jeffrey Sachs, The End to Poverty (London and New York: Penguin Books, 2006), 50

60 Ibid., 33

61 E. L. Jones, op. cit., xxxi

62 Jared Diamond, Guns, Germs and Steel: The Fates of Human Societies (New York: W. W. Norton, 1999), 25

63 Jesse Bylock, Viking Age Iceland (New York: Penguin, 2001), 93–94

64 Vilhelm Moberg, A History of The Swedish People; From Renaissance to Revolution (New York: Dorsett Press, 1989), 74

65 Barbara Tuckman, The First Salute (New York: Alfred A. Knopf, 1988), 90

66 Ibid., 37

67 Geyl, Pieter (1959) Geschiedenis van de Nederlandse stam., 272. Retrieved 7 August 2017

68 Dan Senor & Saul Singer, Start-Up Nation: The Story of Israel's Economic Miracle: (New York: Twelve, Hachette Book Group, 2009)

69 Ibid., 126

70 Ibid., 16

71 Ibid., 17

72 Johan Norberg, The Myth of Swedish Socialist Success (Free Market Foundation, 2016)

73 Ibid.

74 Ruchir Sharma, Breakout Nations (New York: W. W. Norton, 2012), 195

75 Ibid., 246

76 Stanford.edu/entries, Albert the Great (Stanford Encyclopedia of Philosophy. rev. 2/19/20)

77 E. L Jones, op. cit., 61

78 Ibid., 67

79 Samuel Smiles, Lives of the Engineers (London: Folio Society, 2006), 199-200

80 Ibid., xvii

81 E. L. Jones, op. cit., 61

82 Ibid., 67 (CG note 234)

83 Kenneth Clark, Civilization (London: The Folio Society, 1999), 68

84 John Burrow, History of Historians: Epics, Chronicles, Romances, and Inquiries from Herodotus and Thucydides to the Twentieth Century (New York: Alfred A. Knopf, 2008), 484

85 Ibid., 483, 485

86 Ibid., 470

87 Ibid., 477

88 Bertrand Russell, Wisdom of The West (London: Rathbone Books, ltd., 1959), 162

89   Ibid., 162

90   William H. McNeill, op. cit., 691

91   Ibid., 502–3

92   E. L. Jones, op. cit., 203-6

93   Samuel P. Huntington, Who Are We? The Challenges to America's Identity (New York: Simon & Schuster Paper-backs, 2004), 37

94   Ibid., 38

95   Acemoglu & Robinson, op. cit., 26

96   Ibid., 26

97   Ibid., 27

98   Louis Hartz, The Founding of New Societies (New York: Harcourt, Brace & World, Inc., 1964), 73

99   Ibid., 78

100 Ibid., 109

101 Ibid., 80

102 Huntington, op. cit., 40

103 Wilbur Zelinsky, The Cultural Geography of the United States, Rev. Ed., 1992 (Englewood Cliffs, NJ, 1992), 23

104 Jim Rumford, Tobacco, Trusts and Trump, (Brooksville Press), 47

105 James D. Agresti, www.justfacts.com, 8/26/19

106 Ibid.

107 Will and Ariel Durant, The Lessons of History (Norwalk CT: Eaton Press, 2002), 63

108 Ibid., 59

109 Ibid., 17

110 American Action News, February 11, 2020, by AAN Staff.

111 American Action News, When Will Conservatives Understand That It's Not a Contest of Ideas?, January, 22, 2020 by Mark Bauerlein.

112 Mark Mullen, from the Amazon listing for Who Controls America?

113 Mark Mullen, Who Controls America? (Haddon Township NJ. First Edition), 90-91

114 Ibid., 97-8

115 Ibid., 99

116 Christopher B. Daly, How Wilson's Propaganda Machine Changed American Journalism (SmithsonianMag.com, August 28, 2017)

117 Mark Mullen, Nearsighted, What the Elite Want You to See, 2018, p. 67

118 Ibid., 67

119 Ibid., 68

120 Peter J. Dougherty, Who's Afraid of Adam Smith? How the Market Got Its Soul, 1st Edition (New York: Wiley, 2002), 186-7

121 Chairman Alan Greenspan, Remarks at the American Enterprise Institute, Washington, D.C., December 5, 1996, 6

122 Andro Linklater, Owning the Earth: The Transforming History of Land Ownership (London: Bloomsbury Publishing, Plc, 2013), 56-7

123 Ibid., 58

124 Ibid., 19

125 Ibid., 20

126 Ibid., 23

127 Ibid., 70-1

128 Rumford, op. cit.

129 Gary Galles, Before Adam Smith There Was Chydenius (Mises Daily Articles, September 15, 2014)

130 Karl Marx, Das Kapital, 1867.

131 Robert Conquest, Reflections on a Ravaged Century (New York: W. W. Norton & Company, 2001), 75-8

132 Simon, op. cit., 197

133 Nathan Rosenberg & L. E. Birdzell, Jr., How the West Grew Rich: The Economic Transformation of The Industrial World (New York: Basic Books, Inc., 1986), 25

134 Ibid., 24-5

135 Ibid., xi

136 Ibid., 34

137 Anand Giridharadas, interview on The Ink: Elizabeth Warren Says America's Billionaires Aren't Real Capitalists, March 3, 2021

138 G. Edward Griffin, The Creature from Jekyll Island (Westlake Village CA: American Media), 3-4

139 Ibid., 5

140 Ibid., 8-9

141 Ibid., 12

142 William Greider, Secrets of the Temple: How the Federal Reserve Runs the Country (New York NY: Simon & Schuster Paperbacks, 1987), 275

143 Anand Giridharadas, interview on The Ink: Elizabeth Warren Says America's Billionaires Aren't Real Capitalists, March 3, 2021

144 Amand Giridharadas, Interview on The Ink, op. cit.

145 Niall Ferguson, The Great Divergence (New York: Penguin Books, 2014)

146 Ibid., 150-51

147 Ibid., 151

148 Alexander Deane, The Great Abdication: Why Britain's Decline Is the Fault of the Middle Class (Exeter, UK: Imprint-Academic, 2005), back cover.

149 Acemoglu & Robinson, op. cit., 153

150 Ibid, 154

151 Ibid, op., 155

152 Thomas F. Madden, Venice: A New History (New York: Penguin Group, 2013), 178

153 Acemoglu & Robinson, op. cit., 156

154 Arthur Herman, The Idea of Decline in Western History (New York: Free Press, 1997),7 &10

155 Ibid., 451

156 Ibid., 451

157 Ibid., 450

158 Ibid., 450

159 Gretchen Morgenstern and Joshua Rosner, Reckless Endangerment: How Outsized Ambition, Greed, and Corruption Led to Economic Armageddon (New York: Times Books, 2011), 4-7

160 Christopher Hayes, Twilight of the Elites: America After Meritocracy (New York: Crown Publishers, 2012), 175

161 Ibid., 175

162 Ibid., 229

163 Jones, op. cit., 62-5

164 Hayes, op. cit., 168-69

165 Ibid., 168

166 Lyle H. Rossiter, Jr., M.D., The Liberal Mind: The Psycho-logical Causes of Political Madness (St. Charles IL: Free

World Books, LLC, 2006), 328

167 Marc Bauerlein, First Things, When Will the Conservatives Understand it's Not a Contest of Ideas?

168 Greene, Common Genius, Guts Grit and Common Sense (Laissez-Faire Books), 40.

169 Kurt Vonnegut, Galapagos (New York: Dell Publishing, 1999), 207

170 Thomas J. Stanley, The Millionaire Mind (Kansas City: Andrew McMeel Publishing, 2009).

171 John W. Danford, Roots of Freedom: A Primer on Modern Liberty (Wilmington DE: ISI Books, 2000), 176

172 Christopher Ingraham, Washington Post, February 2, 2019

173 Danford, op. cit., 177

174 Ibid., 177

175 Anthony Walsh, A Nation Divided: The Conflicting Personalities, Visions, and Values of Liberals and Conservatives (Wilmington DE, 2019)

176 Scott Adams, How to Fail at Almost Everything and Still Win Big (New York: Penguin Group, 2013), 117

177 Eric Voegelin, The Restoration of Order (Wilmington DE: ISI Books, 2002)

178 Greene, Wasted Genius: How IQ & SAT Tests Are Hurting Our Kids and Crippling America (Lancaster, NH: Lost Nation Books, 2011), 75

179 Forbes.com, Patsy Doerr, The Future of Impact Investing, February 11, 2019

180 Brigit Helms, Access for All: Building Inclusive Financial Systems (World Book Publishing, 2006)

181 Amazon, description of Brigit Helms' book Access for All

182 George B. N. Ayittey, Africa Betrayed (Basingstoke: Pal-

grave Macmillan, 1993), 283

183 Michael Klein and Tim Harford, The Market for Aid (Washington, DC: International Finance Corporation, 2005), 35-6

184 Encounter Broadsides, March 13, 2017, What to do About the UN, (from the description on Amazon Books)

185 P. T. Bauer, Reality and Rhetoric: Studies in the Economics of Development (Cambridge, MA: Harvard University Press, 1984), 17-8

186 Ibid., 67

187 Ibid., 4-5

188 Hernando De Soto, The Mystery of Capitalism (New York: Basic Books, 2003), 172

189 Heritage Foundation, Terry Miller & Anthony B. Kim, 2017 Economic Report, 12

190 Hillsdale College, Imprimis, November 17, 2017, Vol. 46, No. 11, Identity Politics, by Matthew Continetti, 1

191 James Burnham, The Suicide of the West: The Definitive Analysis of the Pathology of Liberalism (New Rochelle, NY: Arlington House, 1964), 287

192 Angelo M. Codevilla, op. cit., 86

193 Hayes, op. cit., 231-32

ABOUT THE AUTHOR

"The Parasitic Role of Elites," reflects Bill Greene's conviction that the best way to learn from history is to apply the case method---by examining actual prior experience to learn what has worked well, and what hasn't. As he puts it, "The Proof of what works and what fails is baked in the pudding of prior human experience."

That is why he has eschewed theoretical approaches and directed his analysis to demonstrated results. "If we want to create satisfactory communities, we must learn from history's wins, so we do not repeat proven failures." He warns the reader to beware of those writers who favor theories, and ignore past results, because they are apt to support failed systems like socialism and communism.

"The author Aboard the Isabella"

The authors passion for history and economics began when he participated in the Program in American Civilization at Princeton University. There he majored in Political Science receiving his AB degree with a Senior Thesis on International Law, and subsequently earned an MBA degree from Babson College with a Thesis on International Economics. He also studied International Law at the Peace Palace Program in the Hague, Netherlands, entered the Doctoral Program at Harvard Business School, and served on its faculty as a Research Associate, publishing over fifty business cases for the International Clearing House of Case Studies.

As a CPA, experienced in financial reporting and taxation, he has served as a director, trustee, and officer for corporations, trusts, and philanthropic institutions. Throughout his career he has pursued an interest in governance by serving in several elected positions at both the local and state levels and by publishing three prior books concerning history and economics. However, he readily admits that a love of farming, sailing, and family has frequently diverted his attention to those more pleasant and rewarding pastimes. He lives in northern New Hampshire, in the White Mountains, with his wife Catherine, a few dogs, chickens, and a herd of Hereford cattle and tries to keep up with his twenty-seven children and grandchildren.

NOTES

NOTES

NOTES